Praise for *The Wolf at the Door*

"*The Wolf at the Door* is a down-home, insightful glimpse into a complex and often heart-wrenching form of elder abuse: when loved ones exploit trust and predators prey on the vulnerable. Drawing from decades of experience, Michael Hackard explains the vagaries of predators' maneuvers and victims' motivations. The book is replete with anecdotes, case studies, and research findings that help readers understand elder financial abuse and the remedies that exist to combat it. Hackard offers an honest appraisal of the legal system's promise and its limitations as well as a candid account of his own wins and losses. It is storytelling at its best— engaging and empowering."

> —LISA NERENBERG (MSW, MPH), executive director
> of the California Elder Justice Coalition

"Fighting elder abuse is a team effort that must involve family, friends, and society at large. The key to fighting crimes against the elderly is knowledge and preventing it from happening in the first place. Written by an experienced and caring attorney, *The Wolf at the Door* gives excellent warnings and tips on how to protect your elderly loved ones."

> —MARK FAIRALL, founder of The Real Faces of Elder Abuse

"*The Wolf at the Door* is clear, concise, and well written. Michael Hackard makes the complex and difficult subject of elder financial abuse easy for the public to understand. The book not only provides valuable information, it also explores the options victims of abuse and their families have."

—NEIL GRANGER, chairman of the California
Department of Insurance Curriculum Board

"*The Wolf at the Door* comes at an important point in our nation's history. Over the next several decades, the country's biggest and wealthiest generation, the baby boomers, will transfer roughly $30 trillion in assets to their Gen X and millennial children. The largest transfer of wealth in history will create a situation that is ripe for elder abuse. As cases of elder financial abuse become ever more prevalent, *The Wolf at the Door* stands as an authoritative and reliable source for families and professionals seeking to deal with this scourge. Elder financial abuse is often challenging to prove, but Hackard gives readers specific tools and practical advice for dealing with it. Imperative reading!"

—DAN COLLINS, court-appointed receiver
administrator for the state of California

"In my experience, 'the wolf at the door' is a real threat. As a financial advisor, I've witnessed the problem of elder financial abuse grow by leaps and bounds. Plus, I experienced it firsthand when a member of my immediate family fell victim to a scam. The financial losses exceeded $100,000—not to mention the loss of pride, self-esteem, and confidence. *The Wolf at the Door* is an all-in-one guide and reference book. It provides helpful tips and strategies for identifying and dealing with situations where financial abuse may be occurring. It also covers the various types of abuse, which helps readers to better protect themselves and their loved ones in the future. Awareness is critical, because prevention is needed at the point of attack. Once money is lost, it is gone forever. I commend Michael Hackard for sharing his insights and perspectives. In doing so, he's helping to stem the rapid growth of this epidemic of crime against our most vulnerable citizens."

—PAUL HYNES, founder of SeniorSafeAndSound.org and president and CEO of HearthStone Private Wealth Management

"Mike Hackard's *The Wolf at the Door* is a terrific study, exposition, and handbook for either the lawyer or the client who wants to understand the strategies, law, and common problems surrounding undue influence and elder financial abuse cases. It is both practical and insightful, and it is a must-read for those who must find solutions to these complex problems. I highly recommend it."

—JOE GENSHLEA, California trial lawyer and mediator

"Required reading for anyone with a loved one who may be unduly influenced by a relative or caregiver."

—STEVE BAKER, former Midwest region director of the Federal Trade Commission and founder of the *Baker Fraud Report*

"*The Wolf at the Door* takes a difficult and emotionally fraught subject (in this case, elder financial abuse) and treats it with the sensitivity that it deserves. On the other hand, Hackard never shies away from addressing the horrors of the subject directly, telling stories of specific cases that are heartbreakingly detailed and honest. His book is a valuable resource for anyone facing the uncertainty of caring for an elderly parent or relative—which, let's face it, most of us will do eventually. It's written in plain English (no confusing legalese here) and structured in a way that never feels like an emotional chore."

—CHRIS DREYER, president of Rankings.io

The Wolf

at the Door

UNDUE INFLUENCE AND ELDER
FINANCIAL ABUSE

Michael Hackard, Esq.

Hackard
Global Media

Book layout © 2017 BookDesignTemplates.com
Cover design by Ivan Popov

Publisher's Cataloging-In-Publication Data
(Prepared by The Donohue Group, Inc.)

Names: Hackard, Michael, Esq.
Title: The wolf at the door : undue influence and elder financial abuse / by Michael Hackard, Esq.
Description: 1st ed. | Mather, CA : Hackard Global Media, LLC, [2017] | Includes bibliographical references and index.
Identifiers: ISBN 978-0-9991446-0-2 (paperback) | ISBN 978-0-9991446-1-9 (e-book)
Subjects: LCSH: Older people--Finance, Personal--Case studies. | Older people--Crimes against--Case studies. | Exploitation--Case studies. | Undue influence--Case studies.
Classification: LCC HV6250.4.A34 H33 2017 (print) | LCC HV6250.4.A34 (e-book) | DDC 362.66--dc23

Library of Congress Control Number: 2017910298

Hackard Global Media, LLC
10630 Mather Blvd.
Mather, CA 95655-4125

Printed in the United States of America

To Lisa—my lifetime love, companion, and spouse.

Teach me to feel another's woe,
To hide the fault I see;
That mercy I to others show,
That mercy show to me.

—ALEXANDER POPE, "THE UNIVERSAL PRAYER"

Contents

INTRODUCTION

"Without a vision, the people perish."
—*Proverbs 29:18*

I'm a baby boomer, born in 1950, halfway between the end of the nineteenth century and the beginning of the twenty-first. I suppose that we baby boomers thought we would never get old—a belief no doubt shared by generations before and after us. We boomers share a collective memory: of Beatlemania, rock 'n' roll, and TV shows as profound as *The Howdy Doody Show*, as inspiring as *The Mickey Mouse Club*, as scary as *The Twilight Zone,* and as lighthearted as *Happy Days*. At one time we were an idealized generation, a fact that is still hard to believe.

Now we are aging. Our youngest members are approaching their midfifties, and our oldest members have reached the magic age of seventy. A large percentage of our parents—members of the Greatest Generation—are now gone. We are more aware of facing mortality and dealing with the loss of our parents. Issues surrounding estates, trusts, and financial elder abuse would have generated little interest from us just twenty years ago. Now some seventy-six million baby boomers are devoting both attention and financial resources to address problems seemingly endemic to our age.

So, other than my age, how did I get interested in doing a book on estate, trust, and elder financial abuse disputes? For one thing, the law practice that I lead has a heavy litigation caseload focused on these issues. For another, personal family history has made me both understanding and empathetic toward those who have suffered from trust and estate wrongdoing or elder financial abuse.

Many years ago, early in my second decade of law practice, my mother's family was affected by elder financial abuse, and the effects have had a profound impact on my life over the years. At that time, the focus of my law practice was on land use law, a distant relative of trust, estate, and probate litigation—so distant, in fact, that I had no idea how to protect my family and challenge the wrongdoer who was harming them.

When the incident occurred, I had the same feelings of ambivalence, frustration, impotence, and injustice that most family members of elder financial abuse victims have. Even the right questions seemed elusive. Who do I ask for help? Will those I seek help from think that I'm greedy and just out for myself? How do I prove that what I'm doing is to protect my relative? Will federal, state, or local legal authorities assist our family to right an obvious wrong? Is it true that a wrongdoer can delay or deny justice by forcing the victim's family to wage a costly, estate-depleting legal defense?

The damage from elder financial abuse isn't just monetary. I've seen how estate disputes split families and inflict deep wounds that may take generations to heal. Such inheritance disputes are as old as history and are even referenced in scripture. Take the following incident in Luke 3:13–14:

> Someone in the crowd said to Him, "Teacher, say to my brother to divide the inheritance with me." But Jesus replied, "Man, who appointed Me a judge or an arbiter between you?" And

He said to them, "Watch out! Be on your guard against all kinds of greed; life does not consist in an abundance of possessions."

The parable of the prodigal son is also rich with layers of human failure, divine mercy, and forgiveness. The story touches on the generosity of a father, an ungrateful son, and the father's continuing generosity in forgiving the son who "squandered his wealth in wild living." The parable offers a poignant reflection on the family divisions wrought by concerns and fights over an inheritance, among other topics.

The stories in this book are my effort to share what I know. I've simplified facts, events, and legal language to bring these stories to life, but the book provides analysis from forty-plus years of law practice, as well as lessons learned over a lifetime. Some of the names, dates, places, events, and details have been changed to protect the privacy of those involved, and to provide a platform for teaching.

Mystery clouds elder financial abuse both before and after an elder's death. It is a crime that is severely underreported; according to a 2003 study from the National Institutes of Health, only about 7 percent of all elder abuse cases ever come to the attention of authorities.[1] The damage to our families, local communities, and economy is substantial. A MetLife study from 2011 put the nationwide cost at nearly $3 billion a year, while other researchers have set the figure several times higher.[2] Getting to the bottom of an injury may be difficult, especially if it is clouded by a wrongdoer's cover-ups and the victim's shame, isolation, or failing memory.

Given all of this, elder financial abuse is often challenging to prove. What are the legal hurdles to a finding of elder financial abuse? California jury instructions provide a first look at what it takes to make a successful case. The Elder Abuse and Dependent Adult Civil Protection Act (EADACPA) identifies a number of criteria that may support the legal basis for a finding of a violation of the act, including the conclusion that

> an individual (and/or his/her assistant) took/hid/appropriated/ obtained/ [or] took the decedent's property; the victim (the decedent) was 65 years of age or older; the taking was for a wrongful use with the intent to defraud or by undue influence; and the decedent was harmed.

The application of the EADACPA elements to any one case may seem confusing and arbitrary at best, or difficult to pin down at worst. The ultimate test of whether there is an actual case of elder financial abuse always depends on facts unique to a case, and how specific laws apply to those facts. In this book, I will describe the situations I encounter most frequently in my law practice, but each case is, of course, unique. My goal is to help you understand the legal basis for elder financial abuse and provide you with some tools for getting the appropriate help.

Am I Wrong to Feel This Way?

Most of the clients and prospective clients I speak with have had a very hard time picking up the phone and calling me. It's not that they don't want help, because they certainly do, and it's not that they don't feel a sense of urgency; they absolutely do. What gives them pause is something deeper and completely normal: namely, a sense of guilt or even shame. The unwritten rules of our society tell us that we should not have disputes over family finances with our relatives, no matter how distant. And those same rules can also keep us silent, even when we know deep down that bad things have happened. All families have their deep, dark secrets, don't they?

Finding a successful resolution to a case of elder financial abuse can seem like a daunting prospect, and I understand the anxiety many families feel at the moment they seek legal help. They may be racked by self-doubt and questions. The circumstances should never have gotten to this point, right? Could we have done something differently? Are we partly or even largely to blame for the elder financial abuse that occurred? If the damage has been done, is there any reason or point in pursuing a course of legal action?

In such cases, the first job of an attorney, in my opinion, is to understand the facts and give counsel as to whether the relatives do or do not have a legitimate reason to be aggrieved. Sometimes people call me with stories that don't meet the threshold for elder financial abuse, and my telling them so can help them come to terms with whatever the actual issues were. It is far better to have an impartial third party consider the facts and conclude that no wrongdoing appears to have been committed than for someone to believe there has been misconduct but never know for certain.

On the other hand, I have also seen cases where massive wrongdoing occurred, and yet the relatives weren't confident that they needed to take any action at all. A non-lawyer cannot easily know if someone broke any laws or interfered with another's rights, so I ask prospective clients to consider their situation from the following standpoint, which is a variation on the Golden Rule: If the alleged wrong had happened to you, would you be okay with it? If the response is "absolutely not," then maybe it bears a closer look.

It is hard to seek justice against family members, caregivers, professionals, or even close friends, and feelings of guilt or shame are natural. "I wish we didn't find ourselves in this situation," is a common refrain I hear, yet here we are. We can either close our eyes to abuse that has occurred, or we can resolve to right a wrong, seek justice, and defend those who could not or did not protect themselves.

You can never change what people think of you, but you can choose not to blame yourself and to accept that you did and fought for what you believed was right. If your gut or "sixth sense" tells you a situation isn't (or wasn't) fair, just, or reasonable, maybe it is worth investigating whether the situation rises to the level of being elder financial abuse.

The Four Elements of Undue Influence

One of the most important elements in demonstrating or proving elder financial abuse is the existence of what the law calls "undue influence." Undue influence means excessive persuasion that causes another person to act in a way that results in inequity. (Likewise, causing someone to refraining from acting may result in inequity.) Undue influence is obtained by overcoming the persuaded person's free will. So how do we show undue influence? Each case is unique, but four criteria always need to be considered:

1. The vulnerability of the victim
Medical records, family and neighbor accounts, phone records, financial records, and photographs may support a finding of vulnerability.

According to the state of California, factors that indicate vulnerability include "incapacity, illness, disability, injury, age, education, impaired cognitive function, emotional distress, isolation or dependency, and whether the influencer knew or should have known of the alleged victim's vulnerability."[3]

In several cases I've worked on, factors have included fear of abandonment, fear of the undue influencer, grief, alcoholism, substance abuse, bipolar disorder, family expectations, cultural expectations, and employment relationships. The issue of whether an influencer knew or should have known of an alleged victim's vulnerability was also present.

2. The influencer's source of power and opportunities for abuse

Under California's Welfare and Institutions Code (WIC), a finding of undue influence requires the influencer's apparent authority to be demonstrated. Apparent authority may be proven by "status as a fiduciary, family member, care provider, health care professional, legal professional, spiritual advisor, expert, or other qualification." Psychologists might describe such relationships as "dominant-subservient."

3. Emotional, psychological, and legal manipulation as undue influence actions and tactics

According to the WIC, the following behaviors may be considered evidence of the influencer's improper conduct: "(a) Controlling necessaries of life, medication, the victim's interactions with others, access to information, or sleep; (b) Use of affection, intimidation, or coercion; (c) Initiation of changes in personal or property rights, use of haste or secrecy in effecting those changes, effecting changes at inappropriate times and places, and claims of expertise in effecting changes."

It sometimes seems like an undue influencer must have read an operating-manual checklist on effectuating undue influence. Isolating a parent, intimidating them, controlling all of their interactions, and cutting off their telephone access are often *de rigueur* behaviors of the influencer. As well, attempting to suppress a parent's loyalty to other children—that is, the wrongdoer's siblings—is not at all unusual.

Wrongdoer lies to a parent about how the wrongdoer's siblings (children of the victim) don't care about the parent and won't call or visit are other common characteristics of undue influence. This is particularly pernicious when a parent's Alzheimer's or dementia, along with concurrent memory impairment, make it impossible to remember visits, calls, or other transactions with non-wrongdoer children. By creating a siege mentality in the mind of a vulnerable person, a wrongdoer makes it far easier for the elderly victim to mindlessly follow whatever the wrongdoer demands.

4. Unfair and unnatural transactions or outcomes

This fourth element concerns the fairness of the action(s) being challenged in court. To determine whether the action was fair, the following evidence is taken into account: "the economic consequences to the victim, any divergence from the victim's prior intent or course of conduct or dealing, the relationship of the value conveyed to the value of any services or consideration received, or the appropriateness of the change in light of the length and nature of the relationship."

Examples of unfair and unnatural transactions or outcomes abound:

- An in-home caregiver promises lifetime care to an elder but fails to fulfill the promise.

- The holder of a power of attorney misuses that power to benefit himself / herself or another friend or family member.

- The holder of a power of attorney seeks to have the elder's IRA transferred to him/her.

- Title to homes, other real estate, bank accounts, and securities are turned over to the wrongdoer.

- The elder's long-held estate plan to split assets equally among his or her children is effectively null and void.

- All past preferences for distribution of the parent's estate have been overcome by the wrongdoer's real-time subjugation of the parent's will.

The Wolf at the Door

"Who's Afraid of the Big Bad Wolf?" is a popular tune that predates the boomer generation. For most boomers, the images of the Big Bad Wolf from this familiar old Disney song are indelible, and we can readily identify with the inhabitants of a house threatened by a wolf at the door. Is the wolf so powerful that our efforts at protection are in vain? Are we strong enough to resist the wolf?

Elder financial abuse is the wolf at the door. Our generation is aging, and with aging comes vulnerability. For this problem to be addressed, however, it must be recognized. Vulnerability aside, it seems that elder financial abuse is so underreported because families affected by the abuse either ignore it or are so baffled by the abuse that their response to it is inertia. It is my hope that this book will help people (including lawyers) identify and protect themselves from the wolf at their own door, or the door of someone they care about.

Necessary Disclaimers

If we were having a face-to-face meeting and you asked whether I was always victorious in winning cases, I would readily admit that I do not have a 100 percent success rate. If there are lawyers who can claim such a rate, I would guess that they haven't taken on many cases or only take on easy ones. I lead a law firm that is fairly well known for what we do. We don't just pursue the easy cases. In fact, we do very challenging cases, and we like doing them. All that said, I'm a lawyer, and it is incumbent on me to provide an appropriate disclaimer:

All materials, stories, law, and conclusions contained in this book are for general information only. The information in this book is not legal advice, should not be relied upon as legal advice, may not be current, and is subject to change without notice.

While practice points and attorney information in this book may include descriptions of successful client representations in negotiated and litigated matters, all case outcomes are dependent on the facts of each particular case. Results will necessarily differ based on history, geography, applicable law, advocacy, circumstances both current and past, and other factors that make our lives both rich and challenging.

I make no predictions or guarantees that my law firm or I would be successful in similar matters. Again, results in any matter are not indicative of same or similar results in other matters.

To the extent that contingency fees are referenced, California law requires that all contingency fee contracts be in writing and signed by both the attorney and client. The contracts must also disclose that the fee is not set by law and the attorney and client may negotiate a lower rate, and they must explain how disbursements and costs incurred in the prosecution or settlement of the case will affect the contingency fee and the client's recovery.

Methods and Tactics of an Elder Financial Abuser

Our families, communities, and state legal systems have worked in recent years to protect our loved ones from elder financial abuse. As well, families with elderly adults share a deep concern about the physical, mental, and financial safety of their loved ones. Elder abusers, however reprehensible, often find ways to circumvent the protections that families and society provide senior citizens. Wrongdoers have their methods and tactics, and it's our responsibility to counter them at every turn. If an attorney believes an abuser has gotten away with hijacking estate or trust assets, the attorney should make the wrongdoer pay under the full weight of civil law. With that in mind, what follows is an analysis of the most common ways elderly Americans are taken advantage of.

The Five Most Common Ways Elder Financial Abuse Happens

Very likely, the cases that I've encountered through my practice mirror the cases of elder financial abuse in the country at large.

Accordingly, here are the most common ways elder financial abuse happens.

1. Caregiver abuse

When a Michigan trial judge dismissed a family's lawsuit against a home care company for sending a caregiver with two felony criminal warrants to care for a man in his eighties, the national press erupted with questions about how this could happen.

In this particular case, the Kentucky-based home care company, ResCare, sent a woman to a retired Detroit-area businessman's house to look after his ailing wife, who had dementia. It didn't take long until the wife's jewelry began to disappear—as well as the businessman's fortune. Court filings estimated the losses to be as high as $1.5 million. The caregiver, if she could be called that, moved the businessman out of his bedroom into the basement of his lakefront home and moved her own mother into the home. The businessman's wife died, and within a matter of months, the caretaker "married" the businessman.

When the businessman's family members finally intervened and removed him from his home, his finances were in shambles. None of his bank accounts had positive balances, nor did he have any working credit cards. He had his monthly Social Security payment—that's it.

The businessman and his family are sadly representative of the widespread abuse affecting our growing elderly population. I have handled a number of cases where predators, posing as legitimate caregivers, quickly took advantage of their elderly charges. This misconduct includes physical and medical neglect, and is often coupled with embezzlement and theft.

The Michigan case didn't work out well. Then again, by their very nature, no abuse case can really ever work out well. Even with a partial financial recovery, the seismic emotional repercussions stemming from misplaced trust don't easily recede.

2. Financial exploitation

Financial exploitation takes many forms. Even though I have been counseling families for decades, I am regularly surprised by some new form of abuse. An incomplete list of malfeasance could include the sale of an elder's medications; grocery bills more attributable to cash withdrawals taken by caregivers than bread and milk purchased for the elder; lawn services for a small yard being billed at $300.00 per week; money being used for gambling fees; medical care and dental care being neglected because of a theft of funds; and assignments of bank accounts into joint tenancy with a wrongdoer.

Most families with victimized elders could readily add to the list of the ways elders can be financially exploited. Vigilance helps. Here are some ways you can remain alert:

- Be very careful and take precaution when hiring caregivers. Simply hiring a caregiver company is not an insurance policy against wrongdoing.

- Watch your elder's bank accounts—particularly withdrawal activity or changes in accounts. Sometimes the horse is out the barn door before you discover bank transfers, but late is still better than never (or a year later).

- Be careful and inquiring if you hear that your elder has been making frequent trips to the bank.

- Be vigilant about watching your elder's mail. We have seen situations where financial information is hidden from the view of the elder and his or her relatives. Beware—this is a sign of great danger. Some financial advisors believe that an elder's credit report should be ordered periodically, reasoning that a questionable report could be a useful "canary in the coal mine." We have also seen cases where perpetrators cashed Social Security checks belonging to their victim. Accordingly, direct deposit of Social Security, retirement, and dividend checks provides some distance between an abuser and your elder's money.

- Review receipts from vendors (grocery stores, pharmacies, Costco, etc.) for goods purchased for your elderly relative. We have seen multiples cases in which wrongdoing was first discovered by this kind of review. A $350.00 receipt from the local grocery store showing a $200.00 cash withdrawal can make even the most oblivious family member suspicious.

- Watch for service scams. New heaters, air conditioners, garbage disposals, or lawn irrigation systems sold at an excessively high premium are not unusual.

- Reverse mortgages can be a blessing or a curse. They may provide a large lump sum payment or a stable, predictable monthly income to senior adults, but money coming in from a reverse mortgage may also be a large and tempting "cookie jar" for unscrupulous caretakers or relatives. More than once I have seen reverse mortgages paid to vulnerable senior adults with questionable capacity, and the existence of a reverse mortgage often isn't discovered by a senior's family until the senior has passed away.

3. Misuse of powers of attorney

Durable powers of attorney can be a potent legal vehicle for ensuring a senior adult's health, legal, and financial well-being is in the hands of a trusted agent. If used with prudence by trusted family members or agents, these powers provide legal protection when and if the senior becomes incapacitated or incompetent. When exercised appropriately, such powers are an unfettered blessing. If misused, however, they can destroy a lifetime of planning.

The effective and prudent use of durable or medical powers of attorney brings no headlines. In the same way, the misuse of these legal privileges is often kept secret and met with incredulity by relatives when discovered.

My firm has seen several incidents where power of attorney was misused at the end of an elderly adult's life to benefit the holder of the power of the attorney. Examples of misuse include the transfer of real property to the holder by negating trust provisions that provide for a different distribution; the seizure of personal property held in safe deposit boxes coupled with later denials of the existence of the property; dramatic changes in bank accounts that are inconsistent with will or trust provisions; and the transfer of title to vehicles.

Some holders of medical powers of attorney have even misused their privileges to prevent family members from visiting the hospital bed of a gravely ill or dying relative. The state of California has recently addressed this issue via legislation, making this kind of abuse much more difficult, but stories abound about how a son or daughter, or grandson or granddaughter, could not visit a dying relative because a stepmother or stepfather prevented the visit. If someone is forced to deal with this issue, he or she should immediately contact a lawyer familiar with elder abuse laws. Medical facilities should also be aware of their limitations of their power in preventing visits.

4. Isolation and freeze-outs

Isolating elders from their families, neighbors, and loved ones is an all-too-common occurrence in instances of abuse. Changed door locks, newly locked front gates, cell phone seizures, failure to answer or open the door to visitors, and unreported removals of elders from their homes are part and parcel of the isolation process. These actions cause family members to fear for the safety of their loved ones and also may create a sense of helplessness. Unfortunately, such conduct is common.

For Californians dealing with isolation or freeze-out abuse, the first step is to call Adult Protective Services; residents of other states should contact their local equivalent. Many local law enforcement agencies also have task forces that deal with such abuse. Civil lawyers skilled and experienced in elder abuse issues can assist with these contacts and can also address such issues in civil filings that include restraining orders and other appropriate measures.

Some words of warning, however: While isolation and freeze-out conduct might be obvious to a family member of the elder, this form of misconduct may not be as obvious to authorities. Criminals and wrongdoers do not usually jump at the chance to admit guilt. While there is no excuse for elder abuse, wrongdoers will readily provide them. Here are some common excuses:

- "I had to keep everyone away because they just upset [the elder]."

- "We had to move Grandpa to Arizona because they have the best medical care there."

- "I had to keep Aunt Bessie away from the phone because she only got upset when she heard from her relatives."

- "Of course I had to keep my dad away from my sisters and brother—they're greedy and they only wanted to get his money."

- "I needed to protect my uncle because he was afraid that his children were going to hit him, push him down, or lock him up in a mental asylum."

Don't expect the isolator to readily admit that she bought her boyfriend a new Harley with Grandma's money, that the house and surrounding area are a pigsty because she's doing meth, or that all of Grandma's jewelry was sold to support her drug habit. You've got to dig at it when your loved one is isolated and you're frozen out. The process can be demanding, frustrating, and anxiety producing. Still, don't turn your back on your elder—*do something* to protect the vulnerable.

5. Unwarranted transfers

First, an acknowledgment: Families often find it difficult to transfer an elderly family member to an assisted living or nursing facility in situations where it is absolutely in the senior's best interest to be transferred. In fact, I'd venture to say that most transfers are absolutely warranted and done with love and care for the senior. It's the unwarranted transfers, coupled with wrongdoing, that can petrify family members.

The common setting for unwarranted transfers is the presence of a family member—maybe a stepbrother or stepsister—who is estranged from the senior's other children and family members. For whatever reason, and by whatever treacherous means, the wrongdoer is able to get the elder into his or her home and amend the elder's estate plan. Once the estate plan is effectively altered, it can be "Katy, bar the door!" for change.

More than once, we have seen situations in which a senior is transferred, against his or her wishes, to a facility geographically removed from other family members. In the meantime, personal goods and family mementos are often discarded or hidden. *These* actions often cause more anger than money transfers. You simply can't replace photographs, family heirlooms, military awards, or personal collections with money. Confiscating family treasures is an affront to the remaining family members—a complete disregard of invaluable family history and a glaring mark of the wrongdoer's greed.

Difficulties abound when trying to address unwarranted transfers. First off, the senior often lacks capacity. So what do we do in this scenario? One way to deal with an incompetent senior is to seek a conservatorship of his or her person and estate. This option can come with complications, however: Does the senior really wish to be supervised by a stranger or even a well-meaning family member? Conservatorships can be expensive and time-consuming. Prospective conservatees are afforded legal counsel from a public defender or a private attorney, and the costs of this counsel are paid from the conservatee's estate. It should be noted, though, that courts are often reluctant to appoint conservators, even for those with considerable impairment. Taking away someone's freedom is not done lightly, even if such freedom increases the person's vulnerability to scams and unscrupulous people.

Detecting the Tactics of Elder Financial Abuse

The sooner elder financial abuse is detected, the better the chances for recovery of estate and trust assets on behalf of the victim. So what are the typical signs or "red flags" to look out for? According to the guidelines of the National Adult Protective Services Association, the following factors should be watched closely to avoid a potential personal tragedy and financial disaster:

- **Liabilities and unpaid bills.** What if an elderly loved one who should have the means to pay the bills every month somehow gets their utilities get shut off? There might be more in play than just a faulty memory—a bad actor may have made off with money from the elder's accounts, leaving the victim high and dry.

- **Surrender of oversight**. Very often we see cases where a "new friend," often a neighbor or opportunistic relative, appears on the scene to offer their "help" in managing the elder's finances. At times, they even succeed in gaining power of attorney. Concerned relatives should closely look into any effective forfeiture of oversight for indicators of suspicious activity.

- **Suspicious withdrawals**. As any good investigator will tell you, follow the money. When financial accounts begin registering unexplained withdrawals or checks made out to "cash," it's time for you to speak with bank employees and get further details on who's making these transactions.

- **Vanishing assets.** Another telltale sign of elder financial abuse is when valuables begin to disappear. Suddenly an elder's jewelry, cash, or financial documents such as stock certificates vanish, and the perpetrator takes to living lavishly, with new purchases of fancy attire, vehicles, property, etc.

- **Changed estate documents.** Wrongdoers who commit elder financial abuse will often seek to legitimize their predatory behavior with the stamp of legality. While exercising undue influence on the elderly victim, they'll "shop around" for any lawyer who will agree to change a will or trust document in their favor. Ask your elderly loved one about any such changes. If you are up against such a situation, it may be time to consult an experienced trust litigation attorney.

- **Creditors come knocking.** Is the elder encountering financial trouble where there should be none? Find out the explanation for any property liens or foreclosure warnings. The reason behind a creditor's claims may be more than just a mistake—your elderly family member might have been financially exploited by an abuser who cleaned out their accounts.

Identifying Financial Exploitation and Scams

As the population of senior citizens in California (and the rest of the country overall) continues to grow, so too will the challenges posed by fraudsters who want to prey on our elderly and steal their money. To help seniors and their loved ones identify and avoid scams, I've compiled a list of the most common ploys, tricks, and tactics financial criminals use against the elderly. Fraud can take on many different forms, but the following schemes are especially typical.

Grandparents scam

A senior will receive a phone call from a caller asking "Grandma?" or "Grandpa?" Through this trick, the caller will cleverly elicit the grandchild's name. Posing as the grandchild, the scammer will then say they've gotten into some form of deep trouble; they might claim to be in jail or stranded in a foreign country. At any rate, it's an emergency, and the grandchild needs help immediately! With the grandparent now upset and ready to assist their supposed grandchild by any means possible, the scammer will ask them to wire money to their bank account, often by Western Union.

To avoid falling for the grandparent scam, don't let a caller drag you into the guessing game, whereby you willingly provide them with the names of your grandchildren or other relatives. If a scammer is more sophisticated, they might research their victim on social media—sometimes they'll run the scam on a platform like Facebook. Call your family members and check on the whereabouts of your grandchildren, no matter how convincing a story you may hear about them over the phone or through social media.

Secret shopper

To your surprise, you receive a check in the mail for several thousand dollars to spend at Wal-Mart or another big-box store. You've been chosen for their secret shopper program! In reality, you're being conned into depositing a bad check. Once you make your deposit, the scammers will ask you to wire *them* a check for the difference between the (nonexistent) funds allocated for shopping and the balance of the check. On top of anything you send, you'll wind up owing money for the fraudulent check you cashed. "Secret shopper" is a nasty scam that leaves its bewildered victims thousands of dollars poorer.

Keep elderly loved ones away from fraud schemes like secret shopper by using the too-good-to-be-true rule: If it seems too good to be true, it is—someone's after your money. That means secret-shopper offers are as good as garbage.

Email scams

Email scams have been around a long time and certainly aren't going away. It's cost-effective for swindlers to send out millions of spam emails, even if they only get one or two responses from potential victims. If you have an email account, you're going to receive these from time to time, even with the best spam filters.

The most notorious email scams are "Nigerian prince letters," email messages that inform recipients that they have been selected to share in an enormous royal fortune in Nigeria or some other West African nation. All the recipients have to do to obtain their riches is wire money to the esteemed "prince" to pay the transaction fee. Naturally, there is no pot of gold at the end of this Nigerian rainbow; the net result is your bank account being emptied.

Another common type of email scam is "phishing." In this scam, fraudsters imitate real websites to elicit personal and financial information. You might very well receive a "bank alert" that seems to be from your bank; the message will inform you that your bank account is overdrawn, you are the victim of identity theft, or there is some other problem that requires you to take action. Often the layout of the email and fake website it directs you to will look convincingly real. The actual purpose of the phishing scam is to get you to enter your bank account ID, password, Social Security number, etc., into the phony website, all in order to defraud you.

In addition to Nigerian prince emails and phishing schemes, you may also receive emails marked "urgent" or with some other indicator of distress. Often they'll appear to be sent from friends and relatives, and they'll contain letters or videos you're told to open. In reality, these are fake messages with harmful attachments—viruses or malware that are designed to infect your computer and steal your personal information. Online criminals can mask their spam messages to make them appear to come from friends, family, and colleagues. The goal is to trick you into opening an attachment that unleashes the scammer's virus.

To steer clear of email scams, the best policy is simply to delete unfamiliar emails and not engage with any too-good-to-be true offers to share in African riches. If you get a "bank alert" email that you're unsure of, check your account online (*don't* click on any link in the message) or simply call your bank to check your account. Also, remember never to open attachments from unknown senders, and be very wary of vague or strange requests from seemingly familiar senders who might actually be identity thieves and con artists.

Investment fraud

Investment fraud is an all-too-common form of elder financial abuse, and scammers find numerous ways to perpetrate this crime against seniors. The first variety of scam is the classic Ponzi scheme. In these cases, elderly clients are recruited into dubious investment ventures promising big returns, but which in reality generate no profit—investment proceeds are actually skimmed from client funds.

Ponzi schemers will pose as legitimate entrepreneurs or investment advisors, sometimes offering victims free meals to attend their "wealth seminars." By the time a Ponzi scheme collapses (as it inevitably will if authorities don't intervene), victims are often left penniless and unable to recover any of the funds they had invested in the scheme. By this point, the perpetrator has likely spent all the money and/or distributed it out as false profits.

It's unfortunate but true that there are also a few bad-faith brokers out there who are willing to defraud their elderly clients. Investment advisors and brokers who violate their clients' trust can sometimes steal for years before they finally get caught. To keep a financial predator from looting your accounts or those of your loved ones, make sure to review the advisor's background through BrokerCheck, a tool offered by the Financial Industry Regulatory Authority (FINRA). It never hurts to get a second opinion on a firm or particular advisor.

Along with Ponzi schemes and outright abuses by bad-faith brokers, also watch out for multilevel marketing schemes (MLMs). MLMs, otherwise known as pyramid schemes and "network marketing," are technically legal business models that require the new member to recruit others into the venture to sell whatever product might be on offer. Senior citizens, at times lonely and in need of companionship, can be especially vulnerable to these schemes, some of which will send them boxloads of products and charge them whether they agreed to the purchase or not. So while MLMs are technically legal, they are often highly exploitative of senior citizens through their deceptive terms and practices.

To steer clear of investment fraud, apply the too-good-to-be-true rule—as always—to investment offerings that boast sky-high returns and near-zero risk; chances are they're a Ponzi scheme. Conduct due diligence and consult a reputable advisor who can help you or your elderly loved ones make sound investment decisions. And stay away from MLM pyramids, the only point of which is to enrich those in the very top layer while exploiting everyone else below them with largely empty promises of wealth.

Telemarketing fraud

Often connected with investment scams are predatory telemarketing schemes, another way fraudsters look to entrap seniors. Many elderly Americans receive several phone calls a week from slick salespeople pitching everything from penny stocks to flimsy-sounding "premium retirement programs" for their portfolios. Quick-talking telemarketers will pressure lonely, confused seniors into "once-in-a-lifetime" investments in dubious or nonexistent oil and gas holdings, foreign currency exchange, real estate, and even "blockbuster" movie productions. Another ploy is to hit up the victim for contributions to a supposed charity. Finally, don't be fooled by con men (and women) who pretend to be calling from your bank, hospital, insurance provider, etc. They're looking to elicit your personal information and commit identity theft against you.

It's sad but true that financial abuse is made easy over the telephone. To prevent fraud, make an express policy to never sign on to anything over the phone. Hang up courteously and make sure to register for the federal government's Do Not Call list. Keep it simple: Never give personal or financial information to unknown callers, no matter who they claim to be.

Repair fraud

Seniors are frequently targeted for elder financial abuse right in their homes through the common tactic of repair fraud. If an elder is forgetful or possibly suffering from dementia, wrongdoers will look to exploit this weakness by overcharging for home repairs and yard work. Sometimes scammers will even come around repeatedly, performing the same task several times over a given period and defrauding the victim in the process. Even unscrupulous auto mechanics have been known to jack up prices for elderly, confused customers and engage in dishonest, unethical practices like changing tires every few months.

Another updated form of repair fraud is the "antivirus" scam, which can be perpetrated in person, online, or over the phone. You might receive a fake email, telephone call, or even door-to-door visit from someone offering to check your computer for viruses. They'll tell you your computer is infected and then "repair" it, charging you for a nonexistent service and possibly even stealing your personal and financial information while they access your computer.

Countering repair fraud might mean going to the doctor and getting an evaluation for possible memory loss or increased confusion. Seniors with conditions like dementia must be protected from financial exploitation, and one effective way to shield vulnerable elderly loved ones from repair fraud is to obtain financial power of attorney. When a responsible younger relative takes on this legal duty, it's sometimes possible to recover funds lost to repair fraud.

Sweepstakes scams

Fake sweepstakes, lotteries, and raffles are a widespread form of fraud perpetrated against senior citizens. As part of the scam, you'll get a flashy mailer informing you of your "incredible" prize winnings, or perhaps a telephone call or spam email saying the same. A fabulous fortune is yours to be had, you're told, and all you have to do to obtain your winnings is pay a phony "tax," "shipping fee," or some other made-up charge. Your Social Security number and bank information might even be required to claim the supposed prize. In reality, of course, the sweepstakes is a scam meant to trick you out of hundreds or even thousands of dollars, potentially putting your identity at risk.

The too-good-to-be-true rule applies to most scams, and ridiculous sweepstakes mailers are no exception. A real raffle or lottery wouldn't require you to pay anything or provide sensitive personal info to access your prize. Sweepstakes offers and other contest "winnings" announcements should be promptly tossed in the trash, and whoever's sending them through the postal system should be regarded with strong suspicion. Seniors should have a trusted loved one help them sort through their mail and identify all such deceptive mailers.

Countermeasures and Heightened Vigilance

What are some initial steps you can take to prevent elder financial abuse? Several measures are available to family members, lawyers, financial professionals, and medical caregivers. Along with basic awareness, coordination and ongoing communication between parties translate to increased protection. What follows are some basic actions you can take to keep elderly loved ones safe from exploitation.

- **Financial oversight.** A family member and a financial professional at the elder's local bank or advisory firm should establish a system of oversight over the elder's accounts. In addition to setting up bill payment, keep a sharp eye on any excessive withdrawals or irregular transfers. Consider joint accounts with the elder, and look into the possibility of a limited credit card for an elder susceptible to financial exploitation.

- **Revocable trusts.** With a revocable trust in place, a trustee has access to bank and securities accounts held in trust. The trustee is subject to California law and the terms of the trust, which outline his or her duties in relation to the beneficiary. This type of trust provides a measure of safety to the beneficiary and remedies for any breach of fiduciary duty by the trustee.

- **Communication.** The human element is vital in preventing elder financial abuse, and that means maintaining effective lines of communication among all interested parties, including the attorney, investment advisor, and/or medical caregiver. Just as importantly, a loving relationship with an elderly family member makes all the difference in shielding them from harm. If a senior is lonely, they'll be more vulnerable to fraud or unethical sales pitches. Just visiting an elder regularly, talking and showing them you care, provides an enormous boost in keeping them safe.

- **No-contact lists.** "Boiler room" telemarketers and deceptive mailers target elders who suffer from cognitive impairment. One way to block most, if not all, of these unwelcome solicitors is to contact the FTC's Do Not Call Registry, Nomorobo, and the Direct Marketing Association.[1] Speak with your elderly loved one about the harmful nature of these calls and flyers to help them spot when they're walking into a trap.

Protecting your elderly family member is virtually a full-time job; indeed, for many people, it becomes a full-time job of care, comfort, housing, medical visits, and protection. We can embrace these duties with love, but it is a love often coupled with real sacrifice.

It is never easy caring for a parent with dementia or chronic physical or mental problems. Both physical and mental exhaustion often accompany such care. Sibling issues can arise between those who are near the elder family member and those who are geographically removed. Friends of the elder might be critical of the care or protections in place for the elder's benefit. Not all is black and white. Taking care of an elder adult often reminds us to reflect on the meaning of the fifth commandment: *"Honor thy father and thy mother."* Doing this honor is a day-to-day process that is not without its challenges.

Tales from the Elder Financial Abuse Archives

As the United States ages and more baby boomers reach senior status each year, the problem of elder financial abuse is destined to only get worse over the next ten to fifteen years. According to the National Institutes of Health, by 2030 there will be sixty-one million people in the United States between the ages of sixty-six and eighty-four, nine million of whom will be eighty-four.[1] If you think elder financial abuse is a problem now, just wait.

The previous chapter highlighted some of the textbook ways elder financial abuse occurs, but you should know that every situation is different. Being wealthy in old age would seem to offer some protection against abuse, as those with financial resources can hire qualified professionals, but, ironically, this is not necessarily the case. Rich or poor, competent or feeble, healthy or bedridden, all elders are susceptible to financial abuse, as the following true stories illustrate.

Police Misconduct

In June 2015, a Portsmouth, New Hampshire, police sergeant named Aaron Goodwin was fired as a result of an official inquiry into an elder financial abuse situation. Goodwin made news headlines for several months after he managed to inherit $2.7 million in property and funds from the late Geraldine Webber, who died in December 2012 at ninety-four.[2]

Goodwin wasn't a relative of Webber's; rather, he "befriended" her in 2010, during a routine house call. The elderly Webber, who had previously been diagnosed with dementia, told numerous witnesses she was "in love" with Goodwin and wanted to leave him everything she owned. Rather than remove himself from the situation, however, Goodwin continued to visit Webber frequently, even taking her on trips to casinos. He then facilitated her wish to change her will, soliciting various lawyers until he found one who would agree to shift $2.7 million in estate assets pledged to the city police and fire departments as well as designated charities over to himself. In the context of the case, Webber's behavior waves the red flags of undue influence, a common method of elder financial abuse.

With Webber's passing, her estate became locked in probate litigation, and Goodwin's claims as the beneficiary came under serious scrutiny. Among other details, John Connors, a whistleblower and forty-two-year veteran of the Portsmouth Police Department's auxiliary unit, spoke out against what he saw as a clear abuse of authority. But no one wanted to listen.

When his wealthy elderly neighbor Webber, already in her nineties, began receiving frequent visits from his fellow officer Aaron Goodwin in 2010, Connors sensed something was amiss. His cause for concern was genuine; two weeks after she met Goodwin, Webber told Connors that the younger police officer had fallen in love with her and would soon leave his wife and children to move in with her, and that she would "give him everything."

By that time it was clear that Webber's diagnosed dementia was manifesting, but what was Goodwin's role? Did he encourage such a delusion through undue influence? The motive for manipulation was simple—Webber bragged that she was rich, even showing her neighbor $30,000–$40,000 in hundred-dollar bills hidden in a silverware drawer. Indeed, Webber's estate turned out to be worth $2.7 million, and Sgt. Goodwin continued to visit the senior citizen practically every day while on duty. In his offtime, he also took Webber on trips to bars and casinos.

Connors continued to sound the alarm on Goodwin's behavior in relation to Webber, but nobody in a position of authority responded. He tried voicing his concerns with higher-ups at various points, only to be greeted with an attitude of indifference or even acceptance.

We are fortunate to have Connors's statements from his February 26, 2015, deposition, which show that he made every effort to alert his superiors to potential wrongdoing.[3] Let's review some of these statements:

- "When I made my complaints to the police department and the higher ups, nobody would listen to me."

- "One commissioner said 'good for them' if the officer and his lawyer could get some of the neighbor's 'ton of money.'"

- "I told [the then police chief], 'You're not going to believe what's going on next door to my house,' the stuff with Aaron Goodwin. I said, 'He's over there all the time,' and he just didn't want to hear it. He just looked at me and kind of smirked and shrugged his shoulders."

- "[The former police commissioner] bends over and he goes, you know what, she's got a ton of money, if they can get in there and get some of it and get away with it, good for them."

- "I didn't want this going public. I didn't want this on the PD, as bad as it was looking, because 95 percent of the guys that work there are the greatest guys in the world. You got a handful that aren't OK, and that's what this is all about."

Once Goodwin shopped around for a lawyer (several refused) who would transfer the bulk of Webber's estate to him just months before her death in 2012, his visits to his elderly "friend" dwindled to around once a week for ten to fifteen minutes. Connors, meanwhile, was served with a notice of complaint from the Portsmouth Police Department that accused him of insubordination, malfeasance, and violation of the department's media policy, but he refused to stay silent.

Standing up and speaking out about known or suspected elder abuse is a brave act, and Connors should have been commended rather than punished. We need to protect whistleblowers who point out a simple truth: the difference between right and wrong.

Was it correct for Goodwin to use his official position to leverage millions from a woman suffering from dementia? The department finally decided that such behavior was unacceptable. Police chief Stephen Dubois (who resigned in 2015) commented:

> This termination is only one of many changes that we have made and will continue to make as we seek to close what has been an unfortunate chapter in the otherwise proud history of the Portsmouth Police Department. We wish to thank the citizens of Portsmouth and the men and women of the Portsmouth Police Department for everyone's patience.[4]

Goodwin was also found to have violated three regulations each of both the Portsmouth Police Department Duty Manual and the city's code of ethics when he helped Webber transfer her estate to him.

In August 2015, a Court finally ruled that Goodwin exerted undue influence over Geraldine Webber by "acting upon her fears and hopes."[5] Like veteran cop John Connors, the courageous whistle-blower who helped bring the story to public light, you can stand up and speak out against elder abuse. Bad actors only get away with wrongdoing for so long—one way or another, they'll be held accountable.

Accountant Fraud

Hiring a professional to manage the resources of an elder does not always guarantee that assets and lives will be protected. Consider the story, straight from Studio City, of Ross and Eunice Bellah. A happy Hollywood couple, Ross and Eunice had been well known in the movie industry for decades. Ross was an Oscar-nominated art director for several famous films and television productions since the 1950s, while Eunice was a painter. Since 1986, when he had already retired, Ross had retained one Aron Shlain as his tax accountant. By 2003, Ross was ninety-six and gravely ill. Shlain convinced his ailing client to appoint him as successor trustee in the event of Eunice's incompetency. A year later Ross died; Shlain bided his time.

In 2008, Eunice fell and broke her arm, and that's when Shlain pounced. He moved her out of the home Ross had designed and built, a Frank Lloyd Wright–style dwelling complete with a Japanese garden and koi pond, and into a convalescent facility. Shlain managed to get two doctors to declare her incompetent, thus gaining control of the Bellah estate as trustee. He then sold the house and adjoining properties for $900,000, reportedly well below market price. The couple's dream home was bulldozed, while the widowed Eunice was confined to a room with an incontinent patient suffering from Alzheimer's.

Neighbor Herb Adelman reported that she "had none of her artwork, no television, no telephone. Nothing." Another friend even alerted California Adult Protective Services after witnessing the conditions Eunice had to live in, but to no avail.[6]

With Ross's widow out of the way, in 2010 Shlain transferred $886,000 from the house sale to his sister in Israel. Eunice's friends went to bat for her in court upon learning about the exploitation perpetrated against her, yet the case dragged on until a Los Angeles County judge finally ruled in 2011 that Shlain had to pay $2.8 million to Eunice's conservator for clearcut elder financial abuse. By then, however, it was too late: Shlain had fled the country to Israel, where he continues to live large off of injustice.[7]

Eunice Bellah died at the nursing home in 2012, a victim of cold, heartless greed. Her friends will always remember her, and those who fought against Shlain's wrongdoing should be commended.

Family Cruelty and Neglect

When a case of elder abuse makes the news headlines, we are shocked at the cruelty inflicted on one of our senior citizens, frequently by members of their own family. Abuse against elders takes many forms, and among them neglect is the most horrific, amounting to the denial of a person's very existence by treating them as if they were already dead.

According to the allegations of the authorities in Redding, California, severe neglect was the reason ninety-year-old Dorothy Havens died on May 15, 2015. Havens had been under the "care" of her daughter Kathryn Jean Havens, fifty-six, and granddaughter Amanda Havens, thirty-three. Dorothy was discovered by police officers the previous night after a report of possible elder abuse, and both her daughter and granddaughter were placed under arrest.

Unfortunately for Dorothy Havens, help came too late. She died at the hospital the morning after her rescue, unable to recover from the abuse she had endured for so long. Investigators say that Dorothy had been in her bed since November 2014 and that she was suffering from bedsores, was covered with feces, and had wounds with fly larvae coming out of them. Her daughter and granddaughter, who were living off Dorothy Havens's Social Security checks, were ultimately charged with murder.[8]

While most of us would have difficulty even contemplating Dorothy's suffering, sadly, her case is far from unusual. Elder abuse and neglect are becoming increasingly more common. There are various motives for wrongdoing, but the results are always the same: irreparable physical and emotional trauma or loss of life.

One comment about Dorothy Havens, offered by her neighbors, stays with us in particular: They "thought she had passed a couple years ago." Elderly victims are often left for dead for by their abusers, and no one notices for years. Dorothy Havens could easily be one of our own loved ones. The simple truth is that elder abuse requires a community solution: neighbors looking out for each other and reporting potential occurrences of this grave crime. We can—and must—do better to protect our seniors.

Not Even the Superrich Are Safe

You might think that being rich and famous would protect you from elder financial abuse, but that turns out not to be true. Consider, for example, the extreme case of Sumner Redstone.

At age ninety-four, billionaire media mogul Sumner Redstone is spending his sunset years engaged in rather unpleasant business: estate litigation. Redstone, the founder of the Viacom and CBS entertainment empires, made headlines in October 2016 due to a spate of lawsuits brought by two former girlfriends who challenged his will and mental capacity, with sums in the millions at stake. He filed a $150 million lawsuit against the women, alleging elder abuse, fraud, breach of fiduciary duty, and intentional infliction of emotional distress.[9]

The first public sign that all was not well in the House of Redstone came in October of 2015, when the kingpin behind National Amusements disinherited lady friend Sydney Holland and confidante Manuela Herzer from his estate. He eliminated Herzer as the holder of his advance health care directive and withdrew the $70 million in assets he had set aside for her upon his death. He also kicked the pair out of his house and arranged for daughter Shari Redstone to make her way back into his life as the new heir apparent to a sprawling multibillion-dollar corporate enterprise. Not one to be pushed aside so easily, Herzer pursued claims of undue influence (based on Redstone's diminished capacity) in Los Angeles County Superior Court, only to have the suit dismissed in May of 2016.[10]

Redstone, his daughter, and their legal team decided to answer Herzer in kind, initiating another round of litigation that will likely leave everyone more miserable aside from the litigators themselves. When Herzer and Holland were ensconced in Redstone's life, the new lawsuit alleges, they convinced him to cash in on Viacom and CBS stock options and treat each of them to a sweet $45 million in cash. This generous gesture, however, left Redstone holding the bag on massive tax obligations incurred through gifting. In addition, Herzer and Holland splurged on shopping sprees from the boutiques of Beverly Hills to the salons of Paris and secured themselves choice real estate.[11]

Based on the accounts of a nurse working inside his residence, Redstone's complaint also alleged that:

- Herzer and Holland convinced Redstone that his family hated him in order to gain more of his estate assets. If they left, they said, he "would die alone."

- Herzer and Holland would use sedatives to keep Redstone from making estate decisions not in their favor and manipulate him into signing documents for their benefit.

- Herzer and Holland would "berate" and emotionally manipulate Redstone to keep him under their control.

If the charges in Redstone's complaint are indeed true, they would constitute clear elder financial abuse. With accusations traded back and forth by all parties, it's hard to determine exactly who has the truth on their side, with the law to back them up. If there's any life lesson to draw from the drama, it's that we might as well concede that unhappy people will use their riches to purchase even more unhappiness. The following is taken directly from the complaint filed by Redstone:

> In the waning years of Redstone's life, as his physical health declined and he became dependent on others for his care and sustenance, Redstone fell victim to financial and emotional abuse at the hands of two women many years his junior, Defendants Manuela Herzer ("Herzer") and Sydney Holland ("Holland"). Beginning in 2010, Herzer and Holland commandeered Redstone's life. They moved into his home and assumed responsibility for his care. They isolated Redstone from family and friends. They terminated his doctors, nurses, household staff, and longtime advisors and brought in handpicked replacements. They decided who came and went from the residence. They spoke for Redstone when he lost his abil-

ity to vocalize. Redstone entrusted Holland and Herzer with all aspects of his personal and financial affairs—essentially everything but his business.[12]

How can we protect our loved ones against elder financial abuse? The stories in this chapter remind us to stand up and speak out and never give up if something is amiss. Set up a system of checks and balances among family members, financial professionals, attorneys, and medical caregivers to ensure that everyone plays fair. No one deserves to be exploited and left for dead—prevent exploitation and stop predators in their tracks.

Elder financial abuse can happen to anyone, regardless of circumstances, even those with supposedly upstanding caregivers and professionals monitoring their health and welfare. The examples I have cited are extreme, but by no means uncommon. Early recognition of elder financial abuse is key to minimizing the damage done, so in the following chapter I will walk through a series of steps I recommend when someone suspects a case of elder financial abuse.

Alzheimer's and Dementia in Financial Elder Abuse

In a report published by the Alzheimer's Association, a full 55 percent of Alzheimer's sufferers and their caregivers said their doctors never told them they had the disease.[1] This seems shocking given the widespread notion that physicians should act in their patients' best interests, but in fact many never provide a diagnosis. Why would there be such a wall of silence around Alzheimer's?

Like dementia, Alzheimer's is a degenerative condition that continues to have a stigma attached to it, a stigma that can even affect doctors. Many doctors aren't comfortable telling their patients their true diagnosis; maybe they're longtime friends, and a range of emotions could result from the announcement, from embarrassment and denial to sadness and anger. Nonetheless, failure to disclose the condition creates a variety of costly problems down the road, from medical bills to risk for elder financial abuse.[2]

Diagnosing Alzheimer's: A Wall of Silence

Whatever a doctor's reasons may be for concealing a diagnosis, such a harmful practice must end immediately. A physician is responsible for providing patients with the fullest picture possible of changes in their health, be they physical or mental. How can an elderly person who suffers from Alzheimer's prepare for future challenges and eventualities without the knowledge they even have the disease? Patient and family unawareness of the disease can be dangerous, and not only in medical situations or everyday circumstances.

If we approach Alzheimer's from the perspective of estate law, we can see that a person's deteriorating mental condition can play a role in faulty decisions, or even worse, leave them vulnerable to undue influence from a predator looking to seize assets. Without a clear Alzheimer's diagnosis made early on, it could be easier for a perpetrator of elder abuse to manipulate their way to control of a victim's estate.[3]

Dr. Pierre Tariot, director of the Banner Alzheimer's Institute, agrees that physicians and care providers need to update their attitude toward discussing Alzheimer's with patients, just as cancer diagnoses today at the very least come with a range of support options and information. Speaking to CNN in response to the Alzheimer's Association's report, Tariot said, "We do need to educate all providers to be aware that hesitance to give the diagnosis reduces the ability of the patient and family to make some choices and planning that is essential for emotional and financial well-being."[4]

Beth Kallmyer of the Alzheimer's Association adds that the major studies in combatting Alzheimer's are directed at the beginning stages of the disease, meaning that early detection is even more crucial. The sooner doctors can be upfront about neurodegenerative diseases like dementia and Alzheimer's, the greater the chances for patient safety and financial security.

An Alzheimer's Victim of Financial Abuse

Undue influence is the most insidious method of elder financial abuse. Whether through isolation, emotional manipulation, or other means, bad actors exerting undue influence abuse their positions of trust and authority for their own benefit. When they discover that a potential target has Alzheimer's or dementia, wrongdoers think they've won the golden ticket.

In a 2015 case out of Arizona, financial advisor John Waszolek wielded undue influence against a victim who was incapable of resisting. The Financial Industry Regulatory Authority (FINRA) barred the Scottsdale broker from his profession after it came to light that he took advantage of a longtime client, an elderly woman suffering from Alzheimer's, by maneuvering himself into her estate as a major beneficiary.

Waszolek, who was working with UBS Wealth Management during the period of alleged misconduct, 2008–2009, learned that his client had been diagnosed with Alzheimer's. Instead of acting to protect her interests, FINRA says, Waszolek decided to illegally and unethically advance his own. In addition to gaining status as his client's estate agent and power of attorney, he "shopped around" for a lawyer who would make him a beneficiary of her trust. Waszolek then stood to inherit $1.8 million, a sum that was originally intended to be split evenly among four charities. Just a day after the trust was amended, he resigned from UBS and moved his practice to Morgan Stanley Wealth Management without informing either of the two companies of his newly secured beneficiary status.

When Waszolek's client died in 2010, he didn't get the big payout he was expecting. The bank responsible for the deceased woman's trust fund would not sanction the transfer to Waszolek's account without approval from his employer, Morgan Stanley. The latter denied that request and ultimately forced Waszolek from his position at the company. But Waszolek wasn't ready to throw in the towel: He then sued the bank, and Morgan Stanley, in Arizona's Maricopa County Superior Court and managed to scrape out a $50,000 settlement. Even so, he ultimately had to answer to FINRA action for his wrongdoing.[5]

The case of Waszolek and his exploitation of his elderly client serves as a reminder that undue influence is more common than we might think. Our seniors are already vulnerable to elder financial abuse, and degenerative conditions like Alzheimer's and dementia unfortunately provide a perfect opportunity for predators to manipulate and force their way into a victim's estate. Setting up a system of verification among family members, financial professionals, and attorneys—thereby ensuring fair play—is an effective way to stop undue influence.

Alzheimer's and Dementia in the Light of Estate Litigation

Busy and experienced trust, estate, and probate litigation lawyers see many estate challenges turn on the nature and effects of Alzheimer's disease on a testator and trustor/settlor. These contests are often fought out in the urban battlegrounds of California's superior courts, not to mention those of other states across the country. Elder financial abuse cases with victims made vulnerable by dementia or Alzheimer's are frequently waged in superior court civil divisions, where jury trials are available.[6]

A 2016 report by the Alzheimer's Association estimated that "610,000 Californians have Alzheimer's disease with that number expected to grow 37.7% to 840,000 by 2025."[7] What's more, the diagnosis of dementia or Alzheimer's is often missed, delayed, or subject to diagnostic error. A 2009 study in the journal *Alzheimer Disease & Associated Disorders* made the following conclusion:

The diagnosis of dementia is initiated mostly on a clinician's suspicion based on patient symptoms or caregivers' concerns, usually in a primary care setting. The diagnosis of dementia in older persons can be challenging in the primary care environment, where provider-patient interactions tend to be brief and patients often present with multiple symptoms and health conditions. Early symptoms of dementia, such as memory impairment, may not be apparent during a routine office visit unless they are directly assessed.[8]

Personal and anecdotal experience leads me to believe that most family members are baffled by an elder's conduct seen in the early stages of dementia or Alzheimer's—a time prior to diagnosis. Those interested in learning more about the disease's early effects should seek out the long and interactive 2016 *New York Times* feature detailing one woman's experience with Alzheimer's, "Fraying at the Edges." The story begins by capturing the confusion that surrounds the disease:

> It began with what she saw in the bathroom mirror. On a dull morning, Geri Taylor padded into the shiny bathroom of her Manhattan apartment. She casually checked her reflection in the mirror, doing her daily inventory. Immediately, she stiffened with fright.
>
> Huh? What?
>
> She didn't recognize herself.
>
> She gazed saucer-eyed at her image, thinking: Oh, is this what I look like? No, that's not me. Who's that in my mirror?[9]

The progression of Alzheimer's is marked by behavioral and psychological symptoms that affect the elder's mental capacity and vulnerability to undue influence and financial elder abuse. Such vulnerability is part and parcel of many will contests, trust contests, and financial elder abuse actions. The story of Geri Taylor in the *Times* describes the disorientation that begins to affect the tasks of everyday existence: forgetting where personal articles have been placed; failing to remember phone numbers, names, and planned events; and losing the ability to do simple mathematical calculations.

Law firms like mine that keep a busy docket in trust, estate, and probate litigation see a common set of circumstances in dementia and Alzheimer's-related cases. For the most part, each case presents a vulnerable elderly victim, a trusted individual who takes advantage of the victim, and an unfair or disproportionate result. Evidence gathered and presented in such cases is often not readily available. To better analyze and understand each individual situation, I have created my own protocol for investigating these cases, the elements of which are outlined below.

- **Time lines.** Time lines are critical in mental capacity, elder vulnerability, and financial elder abuse cases. It may be useful to know that the most critical part of time lines is identifying the time when the first bad act or injury occurred. Such times might be when the elder was isolated, threatened, made dependent, or brainwashed into thinking that everyone wanted to harm the elder except the abusive caregiver or family member.

- **Medical records.** Treating physicians' notes and observations are an important part of a disputed estate or trust case, even though they may not be conclusive. As noted earlier, studies have found that primary care providers regularly delay or fail to make a diagnosis. Also, undue influencers are more likely to present their victim's mental health as normal or only slightly impaired. Given the limited time available in current physician and patient interviews, it's little wonder that a dementia or Alzheimer's diagnosis may not be made even when a more detailed exam would show mild cognitive impairment (MCI) and the onset of early Alzheimer's disease. In any event, testimonies in court or jury trials with competing experts such as forensic psychiatrists and neuropsychologists are likely to conflict. It is a rare case when primary care providers include physicians from such renowned Alzheimer's medical facilities as the Memory and Aging Center at the University of California, San Francisco; the UC Davis Alzheimer's Disease Center; the Mary S. Easton Center for Alzheimer's Disease Research at UCLA; and the Alzheimer's Therapeutic Research Institute at University of Southern California's Keck School of Medicine.

- **Contradictory accounts by family, friends, and caretakers.** If anyone can act as a reliable witness to the progression of Alzheimer's, it's an elder's friends and loved ones. All the same, it's not often that someone in these social categories will maintain descriptive accounts of everything they've seen as the disease takes its toll. Since none of us are perfect, our memories can occasionally be flawed or contradict other facts. Wills, trusts, and testaments taken on video are not very common. Professional caretakers, however, are more likely to keep notes during their work shifts, which means they can more often speak as objective witnesses.

When an Estate File Is Thin on Details about an Alzheimer's Diagnosis

Estate attorneys responsible for the formulation of estates and trusts for Alzheimer's-diagnosed clients must also be classified as important witnesses. When an estate lawyer knows about a client's diagnosis of dementia or Alzheimer's, the lawyer must work to analyze which standards of mental capacity fit with the client's condition and corresponding testamentary documents. It is the duty of the legal counsel to also explain in detail how these conclusions were reached, based on the condition of the client.

A good way to judge capacity is through open-ended questions; the queries and answers can be taken down in the attorney's notes and used to evaluate the client's capacity to make estate decisions. Attorneys must be especially watchful for information that points to undue influence or potential elder financial abuse and ensure that all such evidence is duly documented to protect the client and estate assets.[10]

There are also times when an attorney might not be aware that the client has been diagnosed with Alzheimer's or dementia. Lack of a diagnosis—or one that is hidden, intentionally or not—can be especially harmful, since it leaves an elder vulnerable not only to further medical complications but also to financial abuse and exploitation. If the attorney doesn't document the details of client meetings, including anything appearing out of the ordinary, then an estate or trust might be more easily challenged through litigation when allegations of elder financial abuse or undue influence emerge some time later.[11]

Alzheimer's Disease and Questions of Capacity

When it comes to family members, it's often easy for them to adopt certain frames of mind and perspectives about a relative with Alzheimer's. Maybe they deny the disease or minimize its effects if they stand to inherit most of the estate. A child who acts as a caretaker for some period will be inclined to think they deserve a larger share of the estate and that the parent with Alzheimer's had the capacity to agree to such a decision. All of this must be sorted out by experienced probate attorneys and medical or psychiatric professionals who can analyze the situation from a more objective position.

Capacity is not automatically negated by a diagnosis of Alzheimer's; in fact, California Probate Code Section 811 presumes capacity even if the elder has the disease. Instead of a general diagnosis, state law requires evidence of specific impairments to cognitive functions. Loved ones might believe that the very presence of Alzheimer's disease settles the question of capacity in an estate dispute, but a judge in probate or civil court will demand a more detailed explanation of how the condition created incapacity that then led to elder financial abuse or undue influence.[12]

How Incapacity Can Lead to Undue Influence

Capacity itself is just one element of a trust or will contest case that alleges undue influence, especially when Alzheimer's or dementia is involved. Diminished mental capacity, an undeniable symptom of Alzheimer's disease, leaves a senior in a state vulnerable to undue influence. Opportunistic wrongdoers will jump to grab a bigger portion of an estate or trust than what the elder might have originally planned.

Of course, every case history is unique and requires special preparation. There is no single magic formula that works for litigating all disputed estates or trusts, but the heightened attention given to undue influence and elder financial abuse in California law means that abused beneficiaries and wronged heirs have a fighting chance to protect assets and achieve recovery.

"My Brother Stole My Mom's House"

While Alzheimer's is a tragedy, there are predators who will take advantage of the disease by using it as an opportunity to line their pockets. That can translate to disaster for you and your family. When you've suffered an injustice, you need to right the wrong. If your brother steals the house of your elderly mother who suffers from Alzheimer's or dementia, you're going to demand accountability. In estate, trust, and probate litigation, that means taking the facts and showing how they fit the law. To do this effectively, however, you need expert help. That's where an experienced attorney comes in. If anything less than a knock on the door from the boys in blue can scare a wrongdoer into rethinking his or her strategy, it's a reputation for effective legal advocacy. Forty years of lawyering have provided me with a wealth of experience in representing family members whose inheritances have been taken or threatened by the wrongdoing of one or more family members.

"My brother stole my mom's house" is a common scenario that elder abuse attorneys see. When wronged family members come to me, however, they don't present their concerns in ways that conform to legal jargon. I don't hear about breach of fiduciary duty, statutory elder abuse, or the particularities of probate law. It's our job as lawyers to figure out the law after we've heard the facts. And we appreciate that our clients tell us the facts in their own words, not in a way that's concerned with meeting any real or perceived legal standard.

So do people really say things like "My brother stole my mom's house"? You bet they do. They also say things like "My stepchildren took all of my husband's assets while he was in the hospital"; "My stepmother got my father to disinherit me and to name my stepmother's children as his sole beneficiaries"; "My brother used my dad's power of attorney to take all of my dad's money when my dad was in an assisted living facility and suffering from Alzheimer's disease"; and "My dad is ninety-three years old and just gave his house to his niece who has been his caretaker for the last three months." Of course, I could go on, but you get the idea. These things occur on a regular basis—and for those of us who do estate litigation, such stories are hardly rare.[13]

What do you do if your inheritance has been taken or is threatened by another family member? Here's some guidance drawn from my experience:

- **An estate *planner* is not an estate *litigator*.** This needs some elaboration. There are excellent estate litigators who are also great estate planners—but this is rare. Generally speaking, the rigors, strategy, and tactics required in litigation are very different than those required for the more evenly paced practice of estate planning. The differences in style and comportment required for planning and litigating may be as dramatic as the differences between, say, a mediator and a prizefighter.

- **Get a second and maybe even a third opinion.** This goes for both doctors and lawyers. A specialist in geriatric psychiatry can diagnose Alzheimer's, while a good estate litigator can spot elder financial abuse and undue influence. I have seen meritorious and ultimately successful cases that were rejected by estate planners or other estate litigators. In the same way, I am sure that another lawyer or law firm successfully resolved some of the cases that my firm didn't take— and that's okay. We may have different views as to the viability of a case. Lawyers, like doctors, do not march in lockstep.

- **Take some time to understand your emotions.** We understand that estate litigation is full of stresses, among them a sense of betrayal by other family members or even the deceased. Amidst this betrayal is a sense of guilt. "Am I greedy for even caring about this?" "I should be mourning, but instead I'm angry." "What is an estate dispute going to do to our family?" These emotions and feelings are worthy of reflection.

A lifetime of planning should not be overturned by the undue influence of a relative or some other person who takes advantage of an ailing or already deceased person's vulnerability. Nobody likes vultures. Sometimes the stresses and grief associated with a loved one's passing can cause people to do strange things. That's okay. But what's *not okay* is failing to right wrongs that may have been committed under understandably difficult circumstances.

Working with an Attorney When You Suspect Financial Elder Abuse

A mong its other cruel characteristics, elder financial abuse often leaves its victims defenseless and lacking any means to pursue justice in civil court. On this subject, the words of scripture both inform and resonate:

> Don't take advantage of the poor just because you can; don't take advantage of those who stand helpless in court. The Lord will argue their case for them and threaten the life of anyone who threatens theirs. —*Proverbs 22:22–23*

How does this apply to those who practice law, as well as their clients? It is both a privilege and responsibility to practice law—a privilege that I have now enjoyed for over forty years. A lawyer's responsibilities include the duty to uphold the Constitution and our laws, and to help in the cause of the defenseless or the oppressed.

While every case of elder financial abuse is different, there are common threads among many of them. In particular, these include a strong suspicion of wrongdoing spawned by the isolation of a vulnerable elder, coupled with the guarded and secretive actions of caretakers. As a result of this situation, victims may become despondent that nothing can be done because the matter seems too complex, too far along, or too expensive to prosecute. Many times, potential clients feel that abusers have stripped them of power and funds, thereby making any quest for justice hopeless.

Where others see despair, an accomplished litigator can often spot signs of hope. I don't want to represent that I, or any other attorney, can right every wrong and accomplish the impossible. What I do want to make clear, however, is that what often seems impossible to the inexperienced is, in fact, possible. Mechanics fix our cars when this noise or that bump baffles us. Physicians treat us for conditions that we sometimes can't pronounce or understand. We know that mechanics can't fix everything, nor can doctors cure us of all our ills. Still, we'd rather have their training, experience, and wisdom on our side than not.

When You Need an Attorney

Family members often seek my advice about elder financial abuse or other misconduct well after it has occurred. So, how can victims of wrongdoing fight back when their rights have been violated?

California probate and estate lawyers are frequently after-the-fact witnesses to what brewed in an estate dispute. Once they identify the wrong, probate litigators can then work to fashion a remedy to fix the wrong wherever possible, and for compensation for the wrong when it cannot be fixed.

In cases of elder abuse, undue influence, or even outright estate fraud, family members often sense that there is something amiss even before facts emerge and the full scope of the wrongdoing is known. Visits, telephone calls, and access to the perilously ill family member are either entirely prevented or unreasonably limited. The ailing family member is vulnerable, and his or her loved ones are troubled greatly by their inability to gain visitation access. When the ailing family member passes away, questions about his or her estate are met with silence, delay, or a flimsy justification for the absence of information.

Family members often hesitate to act when they suspect estate wrongdoing. They don't want to seem greedy, and yet in their hearts, they know that greed is not the point. The point is that someone is trying to take their family's estate, be it someone who married into the family, a caretaker, or a sibling.[1]

The very essence of elder financial abuse is the perpetrator's retention of money and assets that either do not or should not belong to him or her. The heirs feel angry. The abuser's acts add insult to injury—think of it as injustice multiplied—and only worsen the emotional pain. If this happens, what should you do?

In most such cases, confronting the abuser seldom produces an immediate solution or benefit. The assets have been moved or liquidated, and the abuser wants to be left alone. Consulting with, and then hiring, an attorney is usually the only viable action at this point.

Finding a qualified and skilled attorney for consultation can itself be a difficult process. There is no perfect method to ensure you make a great choice. That said, I have learned a few things about finding and consulting with people who are superior in their field. Two anecdotes from my own experience may help you improve your chances of securing the services of an outstanding lawyer or law firm.

In 1975, I had the privilege and pleasure to work for California senator Peter Behr. When Senator Behr passed away, the *San Francisco Chronicle* noted that he was a "visionary" who "inspired generations of legislators." While I wasn't a legislator, he inspired me. The senator's widow told the paper that his "greatest asset was his love of people," and his daughter said "he inspired greatness by never focusing on the negative." It is with this background that I can recall the last meeting I had with him, a lunch that he sponsored to celebrate my new job in the research division of the local superior court. The senator wanted to share something with me that I would remember and, when appropriate, act upon.

The senator told me that whenever I had a problem that seemed perplexing, I should seek out and call the greatest expert in the country who could help me solve the problem. He explained that I should simply identify myself as a young lawyer seeking wisdom and knowledge. A short call would do it. Senator Behr told me that the expert would appreciate being recognized for his or her excellence and that in the senator's experience, a person of such preeminence would almost always help. Over the years, I followed the senator's advice, making many calls, and as the years went on, I could no longer claim that I was a young lawyer. Still, the calls were answered even as I reached middle age and a more senior status. The lesson: Whenever possible, start a search by looking for the very best.

Another time, a friend who was a cardiovascular surgeon gave me advice about searching for a physician, but it is just as applicable to finding the right lawyer. My friend advised that when you are faced with a serious surgery, it makes sense to meet with the surgeon, take a notebook, and have a spouse or friend take notes. Have questions written out so that you can seek answers to all the matters that concern you. My friend also advised asking the surgeon how many procedures like the one you're facing he or she performed in the last year. In addition, ask what the outcomes were. I took my friend's advice.

When I was facing a serious surgery, my wife accompanied me to my various appointments with possible surgeons. The first looked chagrined when we told him that we would be getting a second opinion. Then we asked him the question: "How many surgeries like this have you performed in the last year?" He answered one or two. What were the outcomes? "Partial paralysis." It didn't sound encouraging.

We went to a second surgeon. We asked him the same questions. "Over the last year I've probably done about a hundred of the same procedure, I guess—I did two yesterday." Now that sounded better. What were the outcomes? "Good—people recovered well." Now, the other surgeon told me that I might have partial paralysis. "No way—the area that we're operating on would not involve the danger of partial paralysis." Needless to say, the more experienced doctor became our choice. Things turned out well, and I'm thankful for the advice my friend gave me.

When it comes to finding a lawyer, it is wise to start out by seeking out the top practitioners and then getting at least two opinions. Several peer-review rating systems may be helpful for narrowing down your choices, including Martindale-Hubbell® Peer Review Ratings™, Avvo, and Super Lawyers. You will want to look at such ratings, but do not make an ultimate decision based entirely on the ratings. The lessons on excellence that Senator Behr and the cardiovascular surgeon taught me still apply. Those are just places to start your search.

As a practical matter, when people call me about a case, I usually agree to talk for a half hour or so about their case. Many times, the caller lets me know that he or she has spoken with other lawyers. That's fine with me, and I still want to get to the heart of the matter. If I've never done a case like the one described to me, I'll say so. If, on the other hand, it sounds like the kind of case that I handle routinely, I'll say that as well. I always hope that my call will help the prospective client make a decision on attorney selection, and there are a fair number of times that I say, at the beginning or after listening to the story, that I am not the right lawyer for the caller. It has to be a good fit for both the client and attorney. View attorney-client ties as long-term relationships. Indeed, cases can sometimes take years to resolve.

Working with an Attorney:
Hourly or Contingency?

Once you identify an attorney, one more major hurdle remains. Wronged estate heirs and abused trust beneficiaries face the challenge of meeting and paying the real costs of court access, and estate disputes are not cheap. Filing fees, deposition expenses, expert witness retainers, and medical record acquisition costs all add up. Such financial outlays are large even before accounting for the hourly rates charged by lawyers experienced in estate litigation. The simple truth is that trust litigation is expensive, and probate litigators are expensive.

As a litigator myself, I frequently handle trust and probate lawsuits by way of attorney-client contingency fee arrangements. A contingency fee arrangement means that you don't have to pay up front; rather, an agreed-upon percentage of the recovery will be awarded to your lawyer only upon successful completion of your case. Like the special fuel that enables a rocket to take off and reach its destination, contingency fees are vital to propelling an estate or trust litigation case toward favorable resolution.

The very nature of elder financial abuse means that many potential clients have been denied or cheated out of an amount of money or assets; accordingly, they have no way to sustain a courtroom battle to recover wrongfully taken assets and property on their own. This is how a contingency arrangement comes about. Such fees are not set by law and are negotiable between the attorney and client before they sign the agreement.

When I enter into contingency fee agreements, there are some factors that affect the risks I am taking as a lawyer. That is why these agreements are a two-way street: Both the client and the attorney must weigh their interests carefully to achieve a desirable balance between the cost of the case and recovery. I signed my first attorney-client contingency fee agreement in the late 1970s, and my latest one just yesterday, as of this writing.

The firm I lead uses these types of contracts for clients who need a fighting chance. I also ensure they conform to the highest ethical rules and California law. These arrangements also include a section that provides a lien for attorney fees and costs on all claims, causes of action, and amounts recovered as a result of a settlement, arbitration, or trial.

Clients in an estate case usually have a choice between hourly fees and contingency fees. Most individuals, however, do not have the financial resources to cover the necessary costs and attorney's fees required in estate litigation. Contingency agreements are often available for those who cannot otherwise afford to pursue probate litigation. A good litigator will evaluate the scale of the struggle ahead; the nature and size of the case will influence the practicality of a contingency fee arrangement. The percentage of the contingency will vary, but most estate and abused-beneficiary cases are taken by attorneys on the basis of 33 percent to 40 percent of the total recovery; in a few cases, the fee may be as high as 50 percent.

Some Points to Consider about Contingency Fee Arrangements

Contingency fees are an important element of the legal system, and they give individuals greater access to the probate and civil courts. They can also be an effective antidote to the bully trustee or estate wrongdoer who knows that the wronged beneficiary does not have the funds to bring the wrongdoer to justice.

Contingency fee agreements may also be used in situations where wronged heirs or beneficiaries want the executor or trustee to be removed. Additionally, contingency fees can be helpful when recovering assets wrongfully taken by an executor or trustee. Both the attorney and the client in a contingency fee arrangement share the risk of the outcome of the case.

Estates may also hire a probate-litigation attorney to pursue the rights of the estate. California Probate Code Section 10811 permits contingency fees in cases where the agreement between the estate (through the executor or administrator) and the attorney is:

- written and complies with the requirements of Business and Professions Code Section 6147;

- approved by the court following a noticed hearing;

- determined by the court to be just and reasonable, to the advantage of the estate, and in the best interests of the persons who are interested in the estate.[2]

Courts have the discretion to decide the justness and reasonableness of attorney's fees. Contingent fees of forty percent are regularly approved. Moreover, California has developed case law in the area of fee approvals. (For more information on this, see Estate of Guerin (1961) 194 Cal. App.2d566, 575, which affirmed a fee of 50 percent.)[3]

Contingent fees are particularly advantageous to estates as well as heirs and beneficiaries when the client has no money to compensate probate attorneys. They can ensure that extraordinary efforts are taken to determine the validity of wills, trusts, and the rightful owner of real property, as well as the correct beneficiaries and heirs of wills and trusts.

These fees are not appropriate in every case, but in the right ones they are an effective tool for counteracting the information and asset freeze-out engineered by a perpetrator of elder financial abuse.

The Economics of Contingency Fees

Here's the deal: there is a contingent risk factor with any case. The case may not succeed, and in that event, neither the attorney nor the client will get anything. Accordingly, the economics of contingency fee considerations underlie the decision to accept a contingency fee. The client and the lawyer will assess the viability of a contingency fee when they conclude the agreement.[4]

Clients often ask me to consider a contingency fee arrangement in probate, trust, and estate litigation against an elder financial abuser. As a practical matter, one of my main considerations is the amount of the fee in proportion to the value of services performed. It only makes sense to work on a contingency fee basis when the prospective recovery matches the inherent risk factor. A contingency arrangement should be beneficial to both the client and the attorney who earns his or her fee by protecting the client and recovering trust assets on the client's behalf.

Since I face a busy trust and estate litigation practice, I must also consider whether, given the necessary time and labor, my firm can adequately staff and prosecute a new probate and civil litigation case at the local superior court. I have to factor in whether accepting the new case may preclude working with other prospective clients, which is always a difficult trade-off.

While each case is unique, the viability of a professional relationship with the potential client is the critical determining factor for whether or not I accept a case. I turn away plenty of cases where it is evident from the beginning that attorney-client chemistry will be lacking. When a prospective client tells me that his case is a "sure winner," and that all I need to do is exactly what he tells me to do, I go with my instincts and respectfully decline. It's important to understand that successful probate litigation just doesn't work that way.[5]

I enjoy speaking to prospective clients and am always looking for ways to help. That said, initial discussions do not create an attorney-client relationship: Those formalities follow if there is a meeting of the minds and an agreement documenting the relationship.

Lessons Learned

When a client engages me to defend his or her interests, I prepare for battle. In each and every case, I develop plans for tough litigation ahead. Client circumstances always matter. I find the client's story to be the most powerful tool in attaining recovery, and I present the facts of the wrongdoing so that justice can be served. At times, these steps themselves will be enough; confronted with the particulars of the case, an opponent will sometimes seek negotiation and resolution before the dispute hits the courtroom. Otherwise, I'm willing and ready to bring the fight to an estate or trust hijacker and vigorously prosecute elder financial exploitation in civil court.

Even when attorneys are successful in resolving the dispute they were hired for, a client can forget the benefits of the original contingency fee arrangement and challenge the agreement. A protracted legal battle in 2015 over an Alabama estate comprising a valuable coffee company and cattle ranch illustrates this situation well.

It was a classic estate slugfest: four children from the first marriage of a business entrepreneur pitted against their stepmother. Soon after the death of their father, Leroy Hill, the children learned that they would share $675,000 from their late father's $30 million estate; their stepmother would take the rest.

The children hired a well-respected law firm that engaged in a five-year estate fight. At the end of the battle, and after appeals that included an appeal and decision by the Alabama Supreme

Court, the value of the assets recovered for the children was about $33.1 million. To obtain this ruling, the attorneys accrued more than $485,000 in litigation expenses and over 11,000 hours on the case.[6]

The four children then decided to oppose the contractually negotiated contingency fee, which was 40 percent. Circuit Court judge Sarah Stewart heard the dispute. Her words sum up the accomplishments of the lawyers:

> The results achieved by [the lawyers] Kilborn and McDonald are phenomenal: instead of three Hill children sharing $675,000, all four Hill children stand to share in an estate the Hill children themselves recently valued at over $30 million, unencumbered by any personal claim by [stepmother] Debbie Hill . . . [Kilborn and McDonald] accomplished this feat against a team of well-funded highly regarded counsel to whom Debbie Hill paid millions of dollars.

The outcome: The four children lost their effort against the law firm that brought them victory. The judge ruled in favor of the lawyers and determined that the 40 percent was fair.[7]

The judge held the clients accountable for the contractual arrangements that they had mutually chosen—arrangements that motivated the attorneys to do thousands of hours of work and spend hundreds of thousands of dollars. When clients and their attorneys agree to the risk-sharing features of a contingency fee, the attorneys deserve to see their hard work rewarded and the terms of their contract protected.

When a client enters into a contingency fee agreement, it is wise to explore all options. Most of the time I make contingency arrangements because the client does not have the financial means to pursue a trust and estate litigation matter. When a lawyer earns up to 40 percent of recovery on a contingency basis, it can indeed seem to be a hefty fee. Then again, both the attorney and the client started out with nothing, in what is an inherently costly undertaking.

For reference, a discussion of contingency fees such as this one needs to properly end with a special note on how California Business and Professions Code Section 6147 governs California contingency fee arrangements. If you work with an attorney on this basis, note that the statutory requirements are that a fee agreement shall contain:

- A statement of the contingency fee percentage amount.

- A statement as to how disbursements and costs will affect the contingency fee and the client's recovery.

- A statement as to what extent, if any, the client could be required to pay any compensation to the attorney for related matters that arise out of their relationship not covered by their contingency fee agreement. This may include any amounts collected for the plaintiff by the attorney.

- Unless the claim is subject to the provisions of Section 6146 [which deals with claims against health care providers], a statement that the fee is not set by law but is negotiable between attorney and client.

- If the claim is subject to Section 6146, a statement that the rates set forth in that section are the maximum limits for the contingency fee agreement, and that the attorney and client may negotiate a lower rate.

Finally, note that the attorney is required to provide a fully executed copy of the agreement to the client at the time the contract is signed.

Litigation Strategy

Once you hire an attorney and decide to move against an elder financial abuser, battle lines are quickly drawn. And make no mistake: It will be a battle. Disputes around elder financial abuse are always contentious. Accusations and allegations divide families and sometimes cause irreparable separation and the breakdown of lifelong relationships. The hard reality is that there will be winners and losers, and neither party ever comes out completely unscathed.

When I prepare my clients for litigation, I often use battle metaphors to explain that the process of going to court to resolve conflicts bears many similarities to war. Successful litigation strategies are never easy, but the concepts may be simple. Ronald Reagan, when asked about his strategy against the Soviet Union in the Cold War, answered: "We *win*, they *lose*."

The simplicity of this strategy struck the talking heads of the time as unsophisticated, even childish. Looking back at its brilliance, I see how it set a tone and a focal point—a direction for all to follow. The same simple principle holds true for litigation in estate and trust matters.

As Winston Churchill said, "Attitude is a little thing that makes a big difference." When it comes to estate, trust, and probate litigation, attitude does make a big difference. Over my forty years of practice I've come across lawyers who consistently expected to win, and I believe their work, perseverance, and creativity enabled them to win more often than not.

At my firm I apply the "We win, they lose" strategy. This doesn't mean that we *always* win, 365 days a year, or that our attitude alone will save the day. It does mean that I expect to win. I expect that my team's enthusiasm, energy, and experience will translate into a positive outcome. Our commitment to excellence shows.

I do not view myself as a scholar of the law who takes only a dispassionate interest in the outcome of a case. I care about our clients, and I'm here to fight for my clients and protect them. No one hires me to be a law professor.

When it comes to attitude, I subscribe to the philosophy of Charles R. Swindoll, chancellor of the Dallas Theological Seminary. He has this to say about the importance of mindset:

> The longer I live, the more I realize the impact of attitude on life. Attitude, to me, is more important than facts. It is more important than the past, than education, than money, than circumstances, than failure, than successes, than what other people think or say or do.[1]

My mindset boils down to this: I'm hired to fight and win. Now, as a practical matter, not all cases are won outright, and winning ultimately might mean an advantageous settlement. That said, whether involved in estate, trust, or probate litigation, I enter my clients' cases as an advocate, standing tall for my clients and the justice of their cases.

General Litigation Strategy

Like military conflicts, litigation actions have their own context and particularities. Trust litigation is different from bankruptcy litigation, which is different from real estate litigation. That said, most litigation has many more commonalities than particularities, in the same way all kinds of warfare possess a particular nature. All litigation action starts with a plaintiff's complaint and is followed by a defendant's responsive pleading. Discovery ensues, and the long, hard slog toward trial begins.

Whether representing plaintiffs or defendants, litigators must start out with a plan. The uncertainties of litigation soon give resonance to Robert Burns's ode "To a Mouse": "The best laid schemes o'mice an' men/ Often go awry." Experienced litigators give due counsel to their clients that a litigation may not proceed according to plan. In other words, have plenty of contingency plans up your sleeve, because you just might need them.

The number of variables in civil litigation can at times seem endless. Venue counts. Statutes count. Case law counts. Judicial temperament, experience, and calendar pressures count. Witnesses and their veracity, or lack thereof, also count. Documents count. Funding counts. Most importantly, truth and justice should count. Any one of these variables might be the center of gravity for you or your opponent. What it costs to attain justice and have truth judicially embraced is predictably uncertain.

The genesis for uncertainty in litigation is put well by Mike Tyson: "Everyone has a plan 'till they get punched in the mouth." Litigation, like boxing, engages the mind in battle. A series of blows can hurt, change the course of the contest, or just be a part of an unseemly and painful process. Whether engaged in the periodic drama of litigation or the pain of the boxing ring, it is important to "read punches." Punch awareness is much less painful when accompanied by a defensive parry. Even when an opponent's punches are telegraphed, they might still be difficult to parry.

In litigation, as in battle, there are two methods of attack: direct and indirect. As Sun Tzu explained in *The Art of War*, used in combination, these two methods give rise to an endless series of maneuvers. Analyzing these maneuvers, however, could wear us out quickly if we lack the requisite focus for a sustained campaign. Thus was born the concept of zero-based thinking, whereby the best plan for success, in conquest or defense, is predicated upon the best knowledge you have at the moment.[2]

On the battlefield and in the realm of litigation, plans often go awry. A "punch in the mouth" is a dramatic accelerator toward chaos, and thus necessitates a willingness and ability to adapt. Plans, whether upset or intact, will give birth to new plans—and *these* plans lead to an ongoing contest for advantage. The reality of a running estate skirmish can be frustrating for those who hope for a decisive, once-and-for-all battle; like war, estate litigation may ultimately be won by attrition, not brilliant maneuvering.

Successful litigation is fluid and dynamic, and for the strategic-minded attorney, it can play out as a chess match rather than another game of checkers. Nonetheless, be ready for a punch in the face: Your flexibility and preparation will help you to recover, overcome, and win.

Think Long-Term but Be Flexible

Estate and trust litigation calls for a long-term strategy complemented by flexible tactics. Effective litigators must address this complexity at two main levels: the systematic, "big picture" level and the moment-to-moment response level. General Dwight D. Eisenhower captured this viewpoint in a famous quote: "In preparing for battle I have always found that plans are useless, but planning is indispensable."

Estate problems present themselves in different ways. Elder financial abuse is common, as is undue influence exercised on vulnerable elders. Trustee misconduct is also not unusual, and neither is the misconduct of beneficiaries who secured their beneficiary status by wrongdoing. I find that sometimes an early negotiated approach might work, but when it doesn't, Theodore Roosevelt's advice in dealing with adversaries should be applied: "Don't hit at all if it is honorably possible to avoid hitting; but never hit soft!"

Extensive estate litigation experience provides a key advantage. This "in-the-ring" experience has taught me that while an overall estate litigation plan is necessary, success is dependent on the ability to act flexibly through moment-to-moment decisions. Estate and trust disputes are as different as the tactics employed to win them. More often than not, however, I find perpetrators of elder financial abuse and other bad actors to be smug and initially secure that they have covered up their wrongdoing. A flexible—and aggressive—effort to impose accountability on estate wrongdoers, then, can turn the adversary's early smugness into later concession.

Estate litigation is often filed in more than one court. While judges make probate court decisions, juries can make civil court decisions (such as a finding of elder financial abuse). Probate court decisions are often summary in nature and don't include live sworn testimony, while civil courts usually have a longer discovery process, often ultimately leading to a jury trial. Complex cases may be at a disadvantage in a shortened summary proceeding, as deciphering financial records may take far more time than probate proceedings sometimes allow.

When my firm is first presented with an estate dispute, we ask a series of questions. These questions and their answers help us determine an initial strategy—a strategy framed by real-time actions to protect our clients and impose accountability on wrongdoers.

Refuse to Accept the Given

I recently spoke with a fellow attorney who was wondering how to proceed with the civil prosecution of a financial elder abuse case. The lawyer is the senior member of his firm and is experienced, bright, and thoughtful in the field of estate planning. But his professional opinions reminded me that the often linear thinking required of estate planners does not fit well with the battle-informed mindset required in estate and trust litigation.

When it came to estate lawsuits, an area where he had some experience, but not a deep amount, he accepted the given. My experience in law is that the most remarkable lawyers in our field don't necessarily accept the given. Great legal minds often travel apart from well-worn intellectual paths. And I've observed that some outstanding litigators knowingly or unknowingly follow a system called the "OODA Loop," a strategy for action developed by military theorist and United States Air Force Colonel John Boyd.[3]

Boyd's decision cycle is to *observe, orient, decide,* and *act.* Boyd maintains that using OODA allows us to quickly observe and react to unfolding events more quickly than an enemy and thereby "get inside" the adversary's decision cycle and obtain decisive advantage. A colleague of Boyd, Harry Hillaker, explained the philosophy in a 1997 tribute to Boyd in *Code One* magazine:

> The key is to obscure your intentions and make them unpredictable to your opponent while you simultaneously clarify his intentions. That is, operate at a faster tempo to generate rapidly changing conditions that inhibit your opponent from adapting or reacting to those changes and that suppress or

destroy his awareness. Thus, a hodgepodge of confusion and disorder occur to cause him to over- or under-react to conditions or activities that appear to be uncertain, ambiguous, or incomprehensible.[4]

This is a good approach to tough estate, probate, and trust litigation as well. The estate planner would have your actions be entirely predictable—and this predictability would assist your opposition in adapting or reacting to your strategy and tactics. The estate planner desires clarity—and clarity in litigation is akin to popping your head above the trenches to see what your enemy is doing. Such head-popping, suffice it to say, is a recipe for disaster.

Now, I won't reveal how my firm might make litigation strategy and tactics unpredictable. To do so would, of course, make them predictable. That said, I will share some experiences from my legal career and personal life where the OODA loop proved helpful.

Observation

It's the mid-1990s, and I've recently filed a mass of litigation cases regarding Fen-Phen (a diet drug). The litigation is still in its early phase. A number of plaintiffs' lawyers from around the country meet in Denver to map out strategy, and I am a member of the group.

The most serious and fatal effect from the use of Fen-Phen was its link to Primary Pulmonary Hypertension (PPH). PPH is a type of heart disease that has no cure and can cause lifelong debilitation and death.[5] Leaders at the Denver gathering talked about PPH. With great confidence and authority, they declared that there were only thirty-five PPH cases in the country. I quietly observed that they were wrong—big-time wrong. I was already representing three PPH clients, and I'd only been involved in the litigation for a few months. Surely, I thought, there must be many more cases. I acted on my observation, and through information, referrals, and expertise, I ultimately helped dozens of PPH victims. Had I deferred to the authority of the self-proclaimed experts in Denver ("accepted the given"), I would have never represented and helped dozens of people and families suffering from PPH as a result of Fen-Phen use.

Orientation

Orientation "shapes the way we interact with the environment . . . it shapes the way we observe, the way we decide, the way we act," writes Dutch air force commodore and military scholar Frans P.B. Osinga in his book *Science, Strategy and War*. Orienting is the way to build a strategy and employ it appropriately when facing uncertainty and unpredictable change.

I have personal experience with this strategy. It's 1992. I'm forty-two years old, the husband of a loving wife and father of four children. I've got a great family that loves me and that I in turn love dearly. We have many friends, and I've got great clients and a great career. I've also got a brain tumor—shocking news to me and to my family. We prepare for my surgery. It's successful, but I'm disabled for several months. The world is shifting all around us; uncertainty and unpredictable change rule.

We reorient. Family and faith become the center of our lives. We persist. Things are not like they once were. We sell the house we once built with pride and care. Our children thrive, and we follow new avenues in our careers. A medication that I take for the complications from the brain tumor almost kills me. It does kill others.

The FDA orders the drug to be withdrawn from the market. The near-death episode inaugurates a new direction in my legal career: plaintiffs' pharmaceutical litigation. This is a part of my work that I approach with pride and satisfaction. I help many people, employ many people, and make a difference not only for my family but also for the people whom I serve.

Decision and Action

Observing and orienting yourself to conditions around you makes little difference if you fail to make a decision about how to respond to those observations and circumstances.

2011–2012: I've been protecting bank guarantors against lender lawsuits over loans extended before the beginning of the Great Recession. I vigorously defend and represent a large number of clients faced with financial destruction by banks. We do well, and our clients' damages are often limited and settled without a total economic breakdown. The litigation is winding down, and my firm is beginning to wonder what's next.

It doesn't take long before I understand that the graying of my generation, the baby boomers, is creating a new demographic in need of legal assistance and remedies. How do baby boomers and their parents protect themselves from estate and trust problems and elder financial abuse? I decide that this is an area of law that could benefit from my firm's focus and experience and expertise and that we should further develop our practice in this direction. I act on my decision.

My firm now represents dozens of clients in estate and trust litigation during any given week. My geographic practice is focused on several Northern California counties—among them Sacramento, Placer, El Dorado, Solano, San Joaquin, Alameda, San Mateo, Monterey, Santa Cruz, Santa Clara, Marin, and Sonoma—as well as Southern California counties including Los Angeles, Orange, and San Diego. I've developed extensive knowledge in identifying and litigating complex undue influence cases. And I've been a strong advocate of the utility of both the probate and civil courts in effectuating justice in estate-related cases.

OODA—*Observation, Orientation, Decision, Action*—is a continuing loop. The condition of disputed-estate cases is never static. Those who don't understand this will expose themselves to even more risk than what's already typical of probate fights.

Just remember, it's not always wise to "accept the given." One man's "given" is another man's opportunity—and advantage.

Speed Is Your Ally—Delay Is Not Your Friend

Along with the OODA Loop comes another of John Boyd's rules for strategy: "Speed kills." You want speed on your side, not the opponent's. Time should be to your advantage, and with it will come the initiative. In litigation, sustaining a swift operational tempo enables you to file actions, prepare counter-actions, and craft alternative strategies according to your schedule. Be *active*; make your opponent *reactive*.

In probate lawsuits, this principle can be tougher to apply, but it's just as important for a family's future well-being. Addressing financial issues after the death of a loved one inevitably colors grief in ways that anguished family members don't welcome. The heartbreak of loss is exacerbated when surviving family members must choose to take action against a trustee or other estate interloper involved in elder financial abuse or similar exploitative behavior.

It is common to delay a challenge against a wrongdoer trustee. Unless he or she has good reason to be suspicious, a person in mourning won't be inclined to challenge a trustee soon after the death of a loved one. That said, delay has its cost and may have serious financial repercussions. Here are five of them:

- There are short time limits for permitting a challenge to a trust. Failure to act within this time period may complicate and sometimes prevent a claim against a bad trustee.

- Trust assets may easily be diminished or even evaporate if you delay moving against a bad trustee. Liquid assets may be easily moved, and we have often seen bad trustees sell real estate to related parties at prices substantially below fair market value.

- There is a legal concept called "laches" that is described by some as "sitting on your rights." Delays in enforcing rights promptly may destroy an abused beneficiary's rights and remedies against a wrongdoer.[6]

- Quick action with the appointment of a successor trustee—whether a professional fiduciary or a family member—may prevent further wrongdoing and the evaporation of an estate.

- Quick action allows for formal and informal discovery of known and unknown assets.

What is my intake process? I take a call or respond to an email from a prospective client or referral attorney about estate, trust, or probate wrongdoing. Then I gather the facts. Facts likely include probate, estate, and trust documents, copies of texts and emails, and time lines prepared for our initial review. If I take the case, my team will focus on the wrongdoer and the wrongdoing. We get to work; this is not a philosophical exercise. It is an assignment that has real-life consequences for the wrongdoer (and the victim).

If I know the wrongdoer does not have counsel, I have my firm contact him, describe our role, and, usually, suggest a remedy to the wrongdoing. We also suggest that he seek counsel. If he's already represented, I cover the same ground with his attorney. My calls are not full of bluster or threats; they are straightforward. The simple truth is that trust and estate wrongdoing has repercussions. Courts favor early mediation. I am not seeking to exact vengeance on behalf of my client, and all parties may benefit from early resolution. I put our offer to mediate on a tight real-time schedule, and I don't accept excuses for delay. Either the wrongdoer gets it or he doesn't. It is that simple.

I have seen enough circumstances where the opposing counsel's decision to delay is a choice with expensive consequences. I file a civil lawsuit where appropriate: litigation that assures the right to a jury trial, the assessment of attorney's fees, and the possibility of punitive damages. Other remedial litigation may also be filed in the probate court.

The bottom line: A wrongdoer will pay for his delay. It is his choice. My main job is to prevent harm to our clients and to protect them from further harm. If your adversary remembers one thing, it should be that you take your ethical duties seriously and act accordingly.

Trustees: The Good, the Bad, and the Ugly

I met recently with some trust beneficiaries about trustee wrongdoing, and my clients wondered aloud whether I had ever seen anything like the wrongdoing they described. Theirs was a natural reaction to a shocking event that was both inconsistent with their family history and a catalyst for acrimony. Until a once-in-a-lifetime event occurs, such as the death of a sole remaining parent, familial bonds are never truly tested. Once they are, an ugly side of human nature sometimes emerges.

We are often asked, in so many words, what is the law with regard to a trustee's liability for wrongdoing? Here are the fundamentals. According to California Probate Code Section 16400, "A violation by the trustee of any duty that the trustee owes the beneficiary is a breach of trust." Additionally, according to Probate Code Section 16420(a), "If a trustee commits a breach of trust, or threatens to commit a breach of trust, a beneficiary or co-trustee of the trust may commence a proceeding for any of the following purposes that are appropriate:

(1) To compel the trustee to perform the trustee's duties.

(2) To enjoin the trustee from committing a breach of trust.

(3) To compel the trustee to redress a breach of trust by payment of money or otherwise.

(4) To appoint a receiver or temporary trustee to take possession of the trust property and administer the trust.

(5) To remove the trustee.

(6) Subject to Section 18100, to set aside acts of the trustee.

(7) To reduce or deny compensation of the trustee.

(8) Subject to Section 18100, to impose an equitable lien or a constructive trust on trust property.

(9) Subject to Section 18100, to trace trust property that has been wrongfully disposed of and recover the property or its proceeds.

Given the available remedies in most probate litigation for a trustee's breach of trust, the fashioning of those remedies may be both engaging and challenging. Remedy selection is an important part of an efficient and effective probate-litigation practice. Not every wrong requires a full-fledged estate litigation fight; on the other hand, some misconduct is so egregious that ignoring it may imperil and virtually ensure the loss of most, if not all, of the beneficiary's rights to a trust.

Many times, wrongdoing is associated with the abuse of an elder and includes such behaviors as isolation, neglect, and even physical battery. (Emotional manipulation and undue influence are often present as well.) In this regard, California law states:

The elements of a cause of action under the Elder Abuse and Dependent Adults Act, section 15600 et seq. (hereinafter the Elder Abuse Act) are statutory, and reflect the Legislature's intent to provide enhanced remedies to encourage private, civil enforcement of laws against elder abuse and neglect. (See Delaney v. Baker (1999) 20 Cal.4th 23, 33, 82 Cal.Rptr.2d 610, 971 P.2d 986 (Delaney).)[1]

According to California's Welfare and Institutions Code Section 15610.30(a), "'Financial abuse' of an elder or dependent adult occurs when a person or entity does any of the following:

(1) Takes, secretes, appropriates, or retains real or personal property of an elder or dependent adult to a wrongful use or with intent to defraud, or both.

(2) Assists in taking, secreting, appropriating, or retaining real or personal property of an elder or dependent adult to a wrongful use or with intent to defraud, or both.

(3) Takes, secretes, appropriates, obtains, or retains, or assists in taking, secreting, appropriating, obtaining, or retaining, real or personal property of an elder or dependent adult by undue influence, as defined in Section 1575 of the Civil Code."

Additionally, according to Welfare and Institutions Code Section 15610.30(b),

A person or entity shall be deemed to have taken, secreted, appropriated, obtained, or retained property for a wrongful use if, among other things, the person or entity takes, secretes, appropriates, obtains, or retains the property and the person or entity knew or should have known that this conduct is likely to be harmful to the elder or dependent adult.

During a first client interview for a potential estate litigation case involving a trustee, and sometimes for ones involving elder abuse, my focus is on getting the story right. Let's break it down to the basics: What happened? When did it happen? Where did it happen? Why did it happen? How did it happen? Each story is unique, but there are regular patterns that often emerge.

Common Trust and Estate Battles

Below I have identified several of the most common trust and estate battles. This is not an exclusive list; others might suggest further additions or deletions according to their own good judgment. My hope is that this list helps those who may be facing trust or estate conflicts and may help to answer the question often posed: Are we the only family that is facing this kind of problem?

Petition against former trustees alleging wrongful acquisition and misappropriation of trust assets

These cases can be quite messy. Successor trustees to original settlors or makers of trusts are often family members. Putting together a priority list for designation of successor trustees isn't an easy task for the makers of the trust, and the disclosure of the list to children or other beneficiaries is not always met with ready acceptance.

What can happen when successor trustees take charge of the trust? At the death of the trust maker, the first successor in interest is appointed. This can be a readily accepted choice among heirs, or it can be an object of criticism and disagreement. New purchases of cars, boats, houses, or exotic vacations by the successor trustee are an invitation to alarm. We often see the suspicion that trust assets are not being fairly administered—and maybe even wrongfully taken by the successor trustee. We once had a case where the successor trustee bought new cars for her children between the time of the decedent's death and her funeral. It was pretty obvious—and later evidence bore it out—that the trustee had her hand deep in the decedent's cookie jar.

In those cases where family members decide to challenge the actions of the successor trustee, the successor trustee might resign or otherwise be removed from his or her position. Under such circumstances, the new trustee gets to look at the decedent's accounts and determine whether assets were transferred and—if they were transferred—whether the transfers were the result of undue influence or fraud.

The battleground is then set. Were premortem asset transfers valid gifts? Were they the product of undue influence or fraud? Were signatures forged? What was the mental capacity of the transferor? What was the health of the transferor? Time frames for questions regarding mental capacity and health may go back many years. The last series of questions concerns whether the gifts that were made are consistent with the decedent's long-solidified estate plans. Is what happened what Aunt Minnie wanted? If there is evidence that Aunt Minnie had planned over the last thirty years to give all of her estate to her son Buster but she changed her plans shortly before her death to give the estate to her neighbor, it's pretty obvious that something unique and strange went on. The fight is on.

Petition by beneficiaries for instructions regarding interpretation of trust terms

Trust terms are not always clear; there may, say, be a reference to property that is unclear. The distribution of assets to beneficiaries may also be unclear. The arithmetic of estate divisions may not add up. I've seen estates where 50 percent of the estate is left to the sons and 40 percent left to the daughters; the remaining 10 percent was never addressed. Life estates can present particular problems. If there is a life estate, who is to pay for maintenance? Taxes? Insurance? The mortgage? Another common issue is whether the value of gifts made prior to death is to be deducted from a beneficiary's share of the estate.

Petition to compel return of real property to trust, for breach of fiduciary duty, elder financial abuse, conversion, and imposition of constructive trust

This handful of serious allegations can evolve into protracted litigation. These types of petitions frequently arise when the trust maker (or his or her appointed trustee) transferred real property to a new owner prior to the trust maker's death. Examining whether the trustee breached fiduciary duties or took unfair advantage of the trust maker to make a secret profit is part and parcel of these claims. The trustee's duties of reasonable care, undivided loyalty, avoidance of conflict of interest, and preservation of trust property all become points of contention.

Citation to appear at hearing to answer interrogatories (or to be examined under oath—or both)

This is what I colloquially call a "We'll see about that" scenario. I often encounter trustees, executors, or family members who think they can suppress the existence of a trust or will. I suppose they might think that possession is nine-tenths of the law—it isn't. I can bring people into court who have estate-planning documents, and I can have them examined under oath or ordered to answer the questions I pose to them. The availability of this remedy usually cures the document possessor of his or her overconfidence, and the documents are relinquished to our client. In my experience, those who hide a trust or a will usually have a "good" reason to do so—"good" as in the way a car thief has a good reason not to park a stolen automobile in his driveway.[2]

Petition for order removing co-trustee and appointing fiduciary as successor trustee and bringing trust under court supervision

We use this process when there are co-trustees who don't get along for whatever reason. Once you're a trustee or co-trustee, it is not a good idea "to hide the ball." Yet this happens. When we represent an active co-trustee who cannot get information or performance from the other co-trustee, this step comes into consideration. Another part of the process is the appointment of a licensed California fiduciary as the replacement for the errant co-trustee. Probate courts like this approach as an alternative resolution to the paralysis induced when co-trustees cannot cooperate.

Ex parte petition for order suspending the powers of co-trustee (and appointing fiduciary as temporary successor trustee and bringing trust under court supervision)

This has all the attributes of a petition for removal (discussed above), but it reflects an urgency to act. Court rules require a demonstration of urgency for ex parte petitions. In most cases, suspension can occur because of a misuse of assets or because there is a danger of losing assets. An interim trustee (a licensed fiduciary) can come in and help protect the assets during the time period between the fiduciary's appointment and the court hearing appointing a permanent co-trustee.

Petition for order suspending trustee's powers (appointing temporary trustee, compelling a forensic accounting, instructing trustee on real property)

This is similar to the ex parte petition referenced above, but it is generally scheduled for a court hearing two or three months after filing. The unique part of this is the appointment of a forensic accountant to review trust records and account for receipts and disbursements.

Petition to invalidate a trust amendment on forgery and undue influence (no trust funds for legal defense)

It's a nightmare when trust assets are spent defending what ultimately turns out to be wrongful conduct. This type of petition asks the court (and it will require follow-up orders) to prevent the expenditure of trust funds by a wrongdoer. The concept is clear; its implementation is not. There can be skirmishes and all-out battles to stop the payment of trust money for a defense that benefits only the trustee (usually as a beneficiary) and not the trust itself.

The Game Is On

In my experience, once the decision is made to litigate, it is critical to be organized, focused, and aware that litigation itself is not a middle ground or a halfway solution—it is a path to victory. This path may even bring a resolution before trial, but any resolution is possible only because a competent legal team is forging a proper path.

In cases of egregious wrongdoing, it is worthwhile to consider Sean Connery's character, Irish-American policeman Jimmy Malone, in *The Untouchables*. Speaking about the twentieth century's biggest gangster, Malone reflected: "You wanna know how to get Capone? They pull a knife, you pull a gun. He sends one of yours to the hospital, you send one of his to the morgue."

Similar statements are currently being made in discussions about how the Western world should deal with terror groups such as the Islamic State. But estate wrongdoers are not Al Capone, and they're not the Islamic State. Remedies against estate wrongdoers will not involve guns or knives, but the possibility of suing bad actors for punitive damages is the litigation equivalent of bringing a gun to a knife fight.

Litigation is not violent, but its repercussions can change lives—repercussions that *should* have been considered by the perpetrator at the time of the wrongdoing. We are civilized because we have rules, and we endeavor to follow those rules. Innocent people cheated by the wrongdoing of estate predators deserve justice. Punitive damages can punish wrongdoers who have been guilty of oppression, fraud, or malice.

Punitive damage awards are used to both punish a defendant (wrongdoer) and make an example of him or her—an example that the community at large can see. Clear and convincing evidence of malice, oppression, or fraud are necessary triggers to ensure the court imposes punitive damages.

California law defines the terms mentioned above in the following ways:

- "Malice" means conduct that is intended by the defendant to cause injury to the plaintiff or despicable conduct which is carried on by the defendant with a willful and conscious disregard of the rights or safety of others.

- "Oppression" means despicable conduct that subjects a person to cruel and unjust hardship in conscious disregard of that person's rights.

- "Fraud" means an intentional misrepresentation, deceit, or concealment of a material fact known to the defendant with the intention on the part of the defendant of thereby depriving a person of property or legal rights or otherwise causing injury.[3]

If perpetrators of estate fraud are planning to get away with their dirty deeds, they should think twice. All it takes is a skilled veteran litigator to stop them cold and return assets to the rightful heirs.

Removing a Trustee and Holding a Trustee In Contempt

The key to resolving a problem with an incompetent or dishonest trustee is usually to petition the probate court for an order to suspend the powers of a trustee or to remove the trustee of a trust. You would also seek to enjoin the trustee from using trust funds for his or her defense. First, the probate judge grants a hearing. The hearing is held, the superior court grants the petition, and a suspension and/or removal of the trustee is ordered. The court also orders the appointment of the successor trustee. The court will also order the former trustee to turn over all the assets of the trust to the successor trustee. The former trustee is usually ordered to render an accounting to the court within thirty to sixty days of the order.

The successor trustee begins the process of deciphering the financial actions of the predecessor trustee. Questionable money and property transfers are revealed. Now what follows? A variety of petitions and court motions may follow, among them: a petition against the former trustee alleging wrongful acquisition and misappropriation of trust assets; an action against the former trustee to compel the return of real property, and, in the case of elder financial abuse or breach of fiduciary obligation, conversion and imposition of a constructive trust; a petition for an order compelling a forensic accounting of the trust for the time period that the removed trustee managed the trust; a petition to freeze the bank accounts of the former trustee; and enforcement petitions following the former trustee's failure to account.

How does all of this materialize? While there are familiar patterns of enforcement actions against a former trustee, the necessity for such enforcement may be brief, or it may become protracted because of the intransigence of the former fiduciary. The initial part of the process against the former trustee begins with a court order mandating that the removed trustee render an accounting to the court. So what happens if the removed trustee doesn't obey the court order?

On petition of the successor trustee or other interested party, the superior court probate judge signs an Order to Show Cause (OSC) re Contempt, ordering the former trustee to appear before the court to show cause why he or she should not be held in contempt for violation of the court's prior orders. The former trustee must be personally served with a copy of the Notice of Hearing and a copy of the petition.

It is not unusual for the former trustee to fail to account or to appear at the court hearing. The probate court may then impose monetary sanctions against the former trustee and set a new hearing date with an order that the former trustee appear. Next steps follow.

Disobedience of any lawful judgment, order, or process of the court constitutes contempt of the authority of the court.[4] As a result, former trustees may find that their way of doing business in the past does not work very well when they disobey court orders. A violation of California's contempt-of-court law is a misdemeanor, punishable by a fine and up to six months in a county jail.

If you are frustrated with the disobedience of a former trustee to a court order, keep in mind that you do have a remedy that is well founded in the law and well grounded in the court's own need to keep the respect for its orders intact. These matters are rarely resolved without a struggle, but the battle lines are usually clear and the wars very winnable.

The Basics of Proving Undue Influence in a Court Case

When an elder's estate or trust is suddenly changed without explanation to produce an unjust outcome, an unscrupulous family member, caretaker, or another individual could be committing elder financial abuse by the means of coercion known as *undue influence*. Elder financial abuse reveals itself through specific patterns and behaviors, and we can usually track a wrongdoer's steps toward gaining control of an estate. Wrongdoers will employ all sorts of tricks and techniques to get their way: frequent visits, flattery, and gifts (emotional manipulation) as well as isolation, outright intimidation, and even physical abuse. Through these methods, undue influencers can maneuver themselves into legal position for inheriting the elder's funds and property once the elder has passed away.[1]

New documents, signed by the elder under suspicious circumstances, will appear to validate the wrongdoer's claims on the estate. The other children and grandchildren of the elder, meanwhile, are left wondering what action to take after learning that the figurative rug has been pulled out from under them.

The Key Elements of Proving a Case

If you are up against a bad actor exercising undue influence in an estate case, there are certain key elements required to establish your claim. As of January 1, 2014, the definition of undue influence has been updated under California's Welfare and Institutions Code Section 15610.70. Now undue influence claims that are used to overturn invalid wills and trusts in probate court can also be filed in your local county superior court as a potential case of elder financial abuse. Civil court trials, decided by a jury, allow you to pursue damages and punish a wrongdoer for elder abuse. Whether in a probate or civil court, here are the main elements:

- **Coercion.** The division of an estate may indeed be unfair, but if the elder testator is of sound mind and not coerced, then a judge won't take much interest in the result. Unfairness is not enough. What's crucial here is the presence of coercive behavior by the bad actor against the elder. This could be isolation, emotional manipulation, physical abuse, or some combination thereof, all of which produce an inequitable result for the original intended beneficiaries.

- **Burden of proof.** Undue influence provides a legal advantage to plaintiffs, since the burden of proof shifts to accused elder abusers, who are obligated to show they *did not exercise* undue influence. But a plaintiff must first demonstrate: 1) a confidential relationship between the elder and suspected abuser; 2) that the abuser was an active party in forming the will or trust; 3) that the abuser unduly benefitted from the new estate arrangement.

- **Susceptibility.** The mental condition of an elder comes into play when proving undue influence. The elder victim must be susceptible to manipulation by the wrongdoer; in other words, have a weakened mental state. Degenerative diseases like dementia and Alzheimer's, as well as the effects of prescription drugs, can often factor into elder financial abuse stories. Expert medical testimony is necessary to demonstrate elder susceptibility.

All the above elements comprise a viable court case of undue influence and elder abuse. And as with any successful case, a judge (in probate) and jury (in a civil trial) should see the full context and time line of what happened—how a wrongdoer perpetrated an injustice against an elder and the elder's loved ones. Relating the story of what happened in a personal way can be a big step toward holding an abuser accountable and recovering rights to an estate or trust.

How Undue Influence Works: A Practical Analysis

Litigated undue influence cases fill the dockets of California superior courts, both probate and civil divisions. These cases often provide material for examples that I can express best in stories—stories that marshal elements from many cases and are crafted from bits and pieces of my experience gathered over the years, yet are not specific to any one particular case. An example of this sort of narrative follows below. Note that the names in the following story are fictional.

Donna was frightened. In her eighty years of life, she had never been so isolated. She couldn't get a restful sleep, and her checklist of medications challenged her mind and memory. Donna's four children were in their late forties and early fifties. Three of her children led relatively normal family lives, but one child, "Scooter," had a history of substance abuse and problems with alcohol. Scooter had once been married—for six months— but that was decades ago.

Scooter lived with Donna, his mother. More accurately, he lived off his mother. Scooter had not held a job since his pickup- based scrap-metal business ceased at the same time his sentence in the county jail commenced. Scooter's theft of catalytic con- verters from a neighborhood across town came to an abrupt end at 3:00 a.m. underneath a homeowner's car parked in a drive- way. When the county sheriff came upon Scooter after a home- owner's 911 call, Scooter explained that he was sleeping under the car. Scooter's explanation didn't go too far.

Now Scooter, fresh from his fourth stint in the county jail, is at Donna's home. It didn't take Scooter long to convince Donna that his siblings didn't care about her. This wasn't that hard to do, since Scooter would not let his mother speak on the tele- phone with her other children and even went so far as to lock the front gate to protect against intrusion. Scooter's mother put him on all of her bank accounts— bank accounts soon drained by gambling, drugs, and the other vices that Scooter had made a part of his life.

This story can end in a variety of ways. I'll conclude it with a four-part examination of the relationship and actions of Scooter and his mother, with a focus on undue influence.

The vulnerability of the victim

Medical records, family and neighbor accounts, and photographs demonstrate Donna's dementia. Donna expressed her concern that people were out to get her. She seemed oblivious to the way that she had let herself go, appearing unkempt and living in filth. Donna's physical and functional decline were evident when those who had long known her had the chance to see her, an opportunity for the most part prevented by Scooter.

Donna's medications had some mind-altering qualities and also affected her sleep. Donna, oblivious to the toxic mix of alcohol and pills, insisted on her daily vodka and orange juice. Scooter was more than happy to oblige. Outside observers would say that Donna was lonely, anxious, depressed, fearful and still grieving from the loss of her husband.

Donna feared abandonment. Scooter let her know that if he left she would probably be put in an old people's mental asylum. Donna passively accepted Scooter's warnings, but they only increased her fear.

The influencer's source of power and opportunities for abuse

Scooter, Donna's son, was in a position of trust and confidence. Donna's illness coupled with Scooter's enforced isolation and warnings ultimately caused Donna to look only to Scooter for advice and judgment. Psychologists would describe the relationship as "dominant-subservient."

Emotional, psychological, and legal manipulation as undue influence actions and tactics

Scooter seems to have read the operating manual on undue influence. He imposes isolation on his mother and controls all of her social interactions. Scooter has worked to suppress his mother's loyalties to her other three children by lying to her about how they don't care about her, won't call or visit her—which has been made impossible by Scooter. Scooter has created a "siege mentality" for his mother. She now seems to agree to whatever he demands without any critical thought.

Unfair and unnatural transactions or outcomes

Donna lost her property. Her bank accounts are now in Scooter's name. She signed over her house to Scooter. The care once provided by outside sources has now stopped. Donna's long-held estate plan to split her assets between her four children is effectively null and void. All of Donna's past preferences for her estate are overridden by Scooter's real-time destruction of his mother's will.

Deathbed Transfers

Deathbed transfers may be an elder's beautiful gesture of love and care. And who can argue with that? At our life's end, we want to be able to say, as St. Paul did, that "I have fought the good fight, I have finished the race, I have kept the faith." Sometimes deathbed transfers are an important part of finishing the race.

There are other deathbed transfers, and these are spawned not by the love and care of the giver but rather by the avarice and greed of the taker. The taker has a different kind of race in mind: the race to take everything he or she can from the dying person and to keep it from the natural recipients of the elder's bounty. It is these kinds of deathbed transfers that often shake families, fomenting distrust and dissension and ultimately stoking the fires of litigation.

Few would argue that a dying person is not vulnerable. According to California's Welfare and Institutions Code, a dying person's vulnerability is likely marked by "incapacity, illness, disability, injury, age, impaired cognitive function, emotional distress, isolation or dependency."[2] So a deathbed gift is first analyzed within the context of the decedent's overall mental, emotional, and physical circumstances. Once such conditions are understood, the next consideration is whether the influencer knew or should have known of the victim's vulnerability.

It is not uncommon for a dying person to be heavily medicated and alternating between consciousness and unconsciousness. A person need not be heavily medicated to be vulnerable to deathbed undue influence, however. The emotional distress, isolation, and all attendant emotions and concerns of the dying open the door to both the greatest graces and love available in their lives and vulnerability to manipulation by the unscrupulous.

All influencers have some type of apparent authority. Evidence of this authority may include "status as a fiduciary, family member, care provider, healthcare professional, legal professional, spiritual advisor, expert, or other qualification."[3] My firm has seen deathbed undue influence cases involving the coercion of an elder by a spouse, former spouse, caretaker, stepmother, child, niece, nephew, brother, sister, and grandchild. The net of potential undue influencers spreads wide. It's the *abuse* of authority that makes for undue influence.

Undue influence scenarios seem to take hold more easily in families where the elder is isolated from other family members by geography or the intervention of the influencer. Such isolation can be used as a tool to convince the victim that no one loves him or her except the relative or caretaker who is geographically or physically near. The elder might have little knowledge that his or her loved ones have been making continued but frustrated efforts to communicate. Frayed family relationships are the seeds of estate disputes, as these preexisting strains can be manipulated to the benefit of the influencer.

Controlling "medication, the victim's interactions with others, access to information, or sleep" are tools of the undue influencer. Affection, intimidation, and/or coercion are additional tools of undue influence. The undue influencer's actions are often cloaked in secrecy and initiated in haste. Secrecy is occasioned by warnings of dire results to the elder if the secrecy is breached. These warnings often focus on the threat that the elder is going to be put in a home and isolated from everyone that he or she holds dear.[4]

When actions taken by undue influencers are challenged, the scope of the influenced personal property and real property transfers must be fully assessed. Accordingly, discoveries of wrongdoing are often delayed. Real-property gifts evidenced by recorded transfers may be accessed by public records searches, but bank transfers and cash transfers are more difficult. Gifts, grant deeds of real property, assignments of bank and security accounts, as well as changes to the terms of durable powers of attorney, medical and health care powers of attorney, wills, and revocable and irrevocable trusts are part and parcel of many undue influence cases.

Informal discovery in undue influence cases can be quite difficult. Good-faith inquiries into transfers often feed the paranoia of an impaired elder. The elder, already influenced by the wrongdoer, fears that such inquiries will be used to take all that the elder has and put him or her in an "old people's home." Getting over an elder's fears and convincing him or her that such inquiries are focused on the elder's well-being is often a high hurdle.

When undue influence cases are in formal discovery, the "equity of the result" will be one part of the discovery effort. Deathbed dispositions to caretakers made after a long and consistent estate plan benefitting children will be inequitable. The same is true when it comes to preferencing one child or grandchild over another when long-term estate plans favored equity between children or grandchildren. Equitable considerations include "the economic consequences to the victim, any divergence from the victim's prior intent or course of conduct or dealing . . . or the appropriateness of the change in light of the length and nature of the relationship."[5]

Deathbed transfers commonly diverge from the elder's prior intent or years of conduct. I have witnessed several cases where decades of estate planning equally benefitting an elder's siblings, children, or grandchildren are derailed shortly before death—derailed to benefit one sibling, child, or grandchild over all the others. Fodder for disagreement quickly arises in estate disputes between stepparents and stepchildren.

I have also seen several deathbed transfer cases where the elder is speechless, seemingly approving the new estate plan by eye contact or a thumbs-up or thumbs-down. This is an invitation to mayhem. The influencer tells the "deathbed" lawyer that the elder wants this or that; just write it up, and when you visit with the elder you will see that this is what the elder wants. Yes, this really happens. When it happens, family members are baffled as to what to do. For one thing, step back and put this in perspective. Go back to the two-part test of elder abuse.

Deathbed Vulnerability

A dying person's mental, emotional, and physical state is likely marked by "incapacity, illness, disability, injury, age, impaired cognitive function, emotional distress, isolation or dependency."

Might the influencer have known of this vulnerability? In most cases, the better question might well be, "How could the influencer *not* have known of this vulnerability?" That said, the statutory inquiry is whether "the influencer knew or should have known of the alleged victim's vulnerability."[6]

I can think of several deathbed cases where the elder was incapacitated (unable to speak). Incapacitation might be due to a stroke, heart disease, vital organ shutdown, or stage IV cancer (brain, lung, bone, or some other life-ending form). Could this be considered a disability? Yes. Is this an injury? Yes. What is the age factor? An elder. Was this impaired cognitive function?

It doesn't take a professor from Stanford medical school to say yes. Is there emotional distress? Yes. Is there isolation? Yes. Dependency? Yes. Well, it sure looks like undue influence.

What have we learned from all of this? The simple truth is that people are free to give what they have to whom they want. An armed robber is not the beneficiary of this freedom. An armed robber takes by force. A burglar may not be taking by force, but his taking is plainly wrongful. In undue influence cases, freedom is more nuanced. The ultimate question is whether a wrongdoer took advantage of an elder's vulnerability.

Vulnerability, coupled with the influencer's knowledge of such vulnerability, is the primary issue. I don't give much credence to excuses such as "I was only trying to help"; "I was only doing what Uncle Louie asked me to do"; "This is what he wanted"; or "His kids only wanted money."

Undue influence cases are litigation battlefields of emotion, disputed testimony, greed, and often outrage. It helps to have covered this ground before. That said, there are always new ways creativity can be used for ill rather than good. Undue influencers are inventive in their wrongdoing and active in their secrecy. Vigilance is helpful in stopping elder financial abuse, and quick, focused legal action is the best answer to undue influence.

Questions of Capacity

A decedent's capacity at the time of making a will or a trust does not cover or legitimize all estate or financial elder abuse wrongs. This truth is often ignored or misunderstood by estate and trust wrongdoers as well as estate planners who unknowingly participate in an estate plan tainted by undue influence or elder financial abuse.

Probate, estate, and trust litigation has long been characterized as a fight over a decedent's capacity to make a will or a trust. Capacity is just one consideration in determining whether an elder is subject to undue influence.

Elder financial abuse cases can arise from a variety of circumstances. This includes undue influence of a person or entity causing the elder to make agreements, donative transfers, or testamentary bequests to a person or entity that should have known that the property transfers are likely to be harmful to the elder.

Common elder abuse situations involve deathbed transfers, an alcohol-addicted or substance-abusing sibling who uses undue influence to freeze out other siblings from the life or estate of an elder, or the outright taking of an estate's assets.

Whenever litigation seems likely, the defendant's counsel and/or the estate planner are quick to assert that the elder had capacity when the will or trust was made. In fact, in all the litigation that I've undertaken, not once have I heard from an estate planner that when he or she prepared the estate plan, the elder didn't have capacity. This isn't a big surprise. If the estate planner thought that the elder lacked capacity, then he or she wouldn't be preparing an estate plan; it's just that simple. Yet capacity is only one element, and not a dispositive one at that, in determining an elder's vulnerability to elder financial abuse.[7]

California Welfare and Institutions Code Section 15610.70 identifies some (but not all) of the factors that are to be considered in determining the vulnerability of the victim to undue influence:

> Evidence of vulnerability may include, but is not limited to, incapacity, illness, disability, injury, age, education, impaired cognitive function, emotional distress, isolation, or dependency, and whether the influencer knew or should have known of the alleged victim's vulnerability.

In real-life elder financial abuse cases, these factors are identified by procuring the elder's medical records, getting them reviewed by a psychiatrist or neuropsychologist, and soliciting testimony from the victim's friends, neighbors, and family about the presence of other elements of vulnerability.

In litigating these cases, I have watched videos of the decedent signing his or her trust, declarations from a physician or psychiatrist affirming capacity, and the undue influencer's testimony that Mom or Dad always wanted to change her or his will or trust because of some real or fathomed reason. Make no mistake: Mom or Dad can change a will or trust, and the law protects this. What the law doesn't protect is the action of an influencer who uses actions or tactics that constitute elder financial abuse. Among such wrongful actions or tactics identified in the statute are:

(A) Controlling necessaries of life, medication, the victim's interactions with others, access to information, or sleep.

(B) Use of affection, intimidation, or coercion.

(C) Initiation of changes in personal or property rights, use of haste or secrecy in effecting those changes, effecting changes at inappropriate times and places, and claims of expertise in effecting changes.[8]

When I represent aggrieved beneficiaries and heirs, I take a far more aggressive stance if defense lawyers assert that all is well because the decedent had capacity. As previously stated, I have yet to discover a case where an estate planner admits to having prepared a will or trust knowing that the testator or trustor/settlor did not have capacity. A plaintiff's lawyer's inquiries will identify facts that meet the statutes of the Welfare and Institutions Code: vulnerability and actions that prey on vulnerability.

Stepmothers and Estate Litigation

C all it an "Aha! moment." I read the latest summary sheet of our law firm's disputed probate, estate, and trust cases and came across an insight that should have been obvious (but wasn't): About 50 percent of our active disputed-estate cases involve litigated differences between stepmothers and their stepchildren.

Providing an objective assessment of the frequency of stepmother-stepchild probate and trust battles is elusive, but to ignore the phenomenon is to live in another world. For us, the anecdotal evidence is in. In all different cases—will contests, trust contests, life-estate challenges, probate objections, elder financial abuse, deed revocations, or joint-tenancy quarrels—the interests and paths of stepmothers and stepchildren often collide. In California, these collisions play themselves out in the probate and civil divisions of our state's superior courts.

My observation about stepmothers and stepchildren in probate disputes wasn't formed with any conscious design or plan in mind. I suppose that such conflicts are ancient in origin and grounded in the personal motives of each to resist emotional, physical, and financial encroachment by the other. To be fair, stepfathers are not immune to estate and probate disputes; we just find that the frequency of stepfather disputes is a fraction of stepmother disputes. There are some likely reasons for this disparity.

Why Do Stepmothers Get a Bad Rap?

To explain the stepmother phenomenon in estate disputes, let's begin by noting there is a life expectancy gap in the United States between men and women. A man reaching age sixty-five today can expect to live, on average, until age eighty-four. A woman turning the same age today can expect to live, on average, until age eighty-six.

Far more women than men meet the definition of "widowhood"—the status of a spouse who is legally married to someone who subsequently died. There are around fourteen million widowed singles in the United States, and widowed females far outnumber widowed males, 11.2 million to 2.9 million. To the extent that these widowed females and males have stepchildren, it is obvious that the number of surviving stepmothers heavily outweighs the number of surviving stepfathers.

Anyone living in the real world wouldn't be surprised by research showing that only about 20 percent of adult stepchildren feel close to their stepmoms. Moreover, studies show abundant evidence that stepmothers and their stepchildren do not grow closer over time.

Whether the reasons for estrangement are simple or complex, stepmothers' relationships with their stepchildren are often problematic. Even when stepmothers and stepchildren try to develop a positive relationship, a successful outcome may prove elusive. It may not be politically correct to write about the frequency of estate fights caused by disputes with stepmothers. That said, by the time a vigorous estate battle ensues, all litigants' pretensions of political correctness are set aside.

It is said that no two persons ever read the same book. Similarly, stepmothers and stepchildren in contested estates neither see the same facts nor reach the same conclusions in interpreting the facts. Whatever the perspective, an inevitable percentage of estates managed by a widowed stepmother with stepchildren heirs will end up as a battleground of hard-fought litigation over inheritance rights. In my experience, the more heavily lopsided the estate distribution, the more likely there will be an inheritance battle.

Estate disputes grow from smoldering embers, not from sparks that ignite suddenly. Stepmother-family divisions can fester for years. Whatever the source, tensions often exist between members of a first and second family. Even when later marriages are childless, divisions will exist between a father's obligations to his children and his obligations to his later spouse.

Common Elements of Estate Litigation

The trust and estate fights between stepchildren and their stepmothers may seem chaotic, but the facts giving rise to the disputes fit some likely patterns. Let's take a look at some of the common (but not exclusive) elements of estate litigation involving disputes between stepmothers and one or more of their stepchildren.

Marriage term

Short-term marriages present a perfect, brief incubation period for brewing a hot estate dispute. While the decedent's marriage may have been cut short by his death, his long-term estate plan may have been short-circuited by undue influence in the period before his passing. Wills, estate plans, transfers of property, and trusts that are hastily drawn up—with beneficiaries changed during a husband's last days—practically guarantee estate litigation. Claims of undue influence are just about inevitable when a stepmother exerts influence over her dying husband to change all of his estate plans and transfer all of his property to her. Such changes incense those family members who are not only excluded from the will but who were often cut off from visitation during their father's final months or days.

Although long-term marriages don't necessarily provide a safe harbor against an estate challenge, such unions are more likely to have produced estate plans that balance the welfare of a father's children with the welfare of his later spouse. Estate plans in such marriages are usually consistent, and they only run into a challenge when the consistency is interrupted by drastic estate plan changes made on the deathbed or during a final illness.

Stepmothers and estate law: a typical case

The case below is presented to help identify some of the common factors in stepmother-stepchildren disputes. The case, which is painted in broad brushstrokes, should not be interpreted as impugning stepmothers in general, nor impugning those stepmothers who've found themselves in estate litigation. Readers can draw their own conclusions as to why a significant percentage of estate fights involve stepmothers.

Stepmothers involved in estate litigation are often several years the junior of a successful man (a professional, entrepreneur, educator, investor, etc.; we'll call him "Mr. Successful"). Mr. Successful has at least one child from a prior marriage. His child has been a part of his life, at times intermittently, leading to periods of estrangement the child attributes to the stepmother.

Mr. Successful's estate has grown over the years. He's made gifts to his children, and when applicable, to his second wife's children by a prior marriage. Unfortunately, though, there have been tensions in the family. One child (of the father or step-mother) has a substance abuse problem. The problem is either obvious (the child ends up in jail), not so obvious (the child doesn't work, and no one knows why), or ignored (the child has cultivated a one-of-a-kind marijuana plantation in the neighbor's backyard).

There may be a most-favored child. Favored children may be the offspring of the father or the stepmother. Favored children of the stepmother can be particularly problematic. Continual be-hind-the-scenes efforts by a stepmother to advance the interests of her child over those of her husband's biological child won't escape the notice of other family members. Financial favors can include loans, free rent, cars, and vacations. Family members will discover these favors after Mr. Successful's death: not through open disclosure by a stepmother but more likely through records uncovered by stepchildren.

Stepmother disputes will frequently break out immediately upon a father's death. Many times, my firm has seen conflicts over where the deceased's body will end up. Such tensions strike at the heart and soul of family relationships. Where the father was first widowed and then remarried, issues like burial with his first wife will arise. Some stepmothers accede to this without controversy, while others ignore the children's requests and control the burial or cremation of the decedent. Terrible things can occur here, among them the refusal to release "cre-mains" to children, or the refusal to provide a headstone or let anyone else provide a headstone for the decedent. At times stepmothers hide all information about the burial, so that family members have no idea where the remains of their loved one are located.

I should emphasize that such disputes are neither uncommon nor easily resolved.

Hide-and-seek

Hide-and-seek may have been a fun game during our childhood, but it's not so fun when we are grown-ups. Hide-and-seek in the stepmother-stepchildren relationship often begins with a married father's initial affair with a woman destined to later be his wife—more importantly, his children's stepmother. The natural strains between a stepmother and her stepchildren come under even more strain from the stepchildren's feelings of family betrayal, and the stepmother is an easy mark as the source of betrayal. Hide-and-seek may also involve the fact of the father's death. Many times I have heard from families that they didn't even know about their father's death until several days or a few weeks passed. This failure to inform children is reprehensible and a reliable sign that something is being hidden. A lack of information about the location of a funeral, urn, or burial is par for the course in these postmortem hide-and-seek games.[1]

The dementia gambit

Dementia is a general term that embraces a broad array of chronic symptoms due to disease or injury: memory loss, impaired judgment, language difficulties, and personality changes, coupled with reduced powers of reasoning. Family members often shy away from a diagnosis of dementia while their loved one is living. Dementia is a medical diagnosis rife with heavy emotional consequences, which is why recognition of the disease often gets delayed.

Professionals use the Clinical Dementia Rating (CDR) to evaluate the progression of symptoms in patients with dementia. The CDR ranges from 0 to 3, with 0 designated as a normal, healthy state and 3 as one characterized by severe dementia.[2] My experience in estate litigation leads me to conclude that most undue influence activities later challenged in court occur when the elder is at stage 2 or 3 on the CDR scale. In estate litigation, we analyze medical records and conduct witness interviews to make initial, but not final, conclusions as to where and at what point the decedent fit onto the CDR scale.

CDR Stage 2 is when the elder is becoming more disoriented as to time and space. The elder gets lost easily and struggles with time relationships. Short-term memory is substantially impaired. It is at this stage that the elder might not know the month or year in which he is being interviewed. Other confusion may exist as to his relationships; he may think that his sister is his daughter or his spouse is his sister. Disorientation is clear for others to see.

CDR Stage 3 is the final and most severe phase of dementia. Now the elder functions only with assistance from a caregiver. The elder has extreme memory loss. There is little or no understanding of orientation in time or geography. The elder finds it nearly impossible to be a social part of regular activities. Help is required for all personal needs. This is a dangerous time. Household items like stoves, garbage disposals, and hot water can be accidents waiting to happen.

Bad actors can try to exploit the vulnerabilities of an elder with dementia, a scheme we call the "dementia gambit." A gambit is an action carrying a degree of risk that is calculated to gain an advantage. Loosely put, dementia gambits are efforts to unduly influence the elder to engage in an act that might on its face appear to be brazen, but which is meant to take control of a family fortune. Such gambits are common in heated stepmother-stepchildren disputes.

The property-transfer gambit is an effort to have the individual with dementia sign over deeds, powers of attorney, bank deposits, or other assets to a person exercising undue influence. It would be unfair to consign such conduct solely to stepmothers. After all, I have seen similar behavior within the scope of all family members, as well as neighbors, caretakers, and near strangers. But since I've been talking about stepmothers, I will continue analyzing their role in estate disputes.

The telltale funeral

Financial concerns, however unwanted, arise when final arrangements are being made. Who pays for the funeral? For cremation? Burial? Legal concerns over accounts and financial commitments are unfortunately a part of the mix during a time of grief. It is often at this moment that signs of wrongdoing begin to show.

Sometimes hints of wrongdoing are subtle. Other times the hints are as obvious as the proverbial skunk at the garden party. Whether obvious or otherwise, information that should be shared is not. Questions as to the existence or nonexistence of estate planning documents are shunted aside. Often personal property disappears or is signed over into the wrong hands. Precious family heirlooms might be found in the garbage at the decedent's house—sometimes as early as the date of death.[3] It's as though vultures have swooped down on the grief of the innocent. The family home is locked up, the locks are changed, and no one save the controlling party is allowed access.

Blended Families and Estate Tug-of-War

Imagine you're sitting in the probate department of your county's superior court. The couple to your right is whispering that their stepsister is only in court for her stepfather's money. The middle-aged man to your left is busy writing notes to his lawyer about his half sister's efforts to freeze him out of his mother's estate. Attorneys at the counsel tables are arguing over whether the decedent's stepson was a valid beneficiary in a trust. The case heard before the current one involved an elder with dementia giving away all of his assets to his daughters shortly before his death.

You wonder: With all of these upsetting stories in court, do any families actually have estate plans that don't cause bickering and challenge?

As an estate litigator and probate attorney, I've met many clients who are shocked by the seeming necessity of estate litigation. I wish that their now-deceased relative had gotten—or maybe taken—better advice.

I see some of the same mistakes and estate battles again and again, particularly when heirs include siblings, stepsiblings, half siblings, and/or stepparents. Categorizing some of the repetitive issues families face can help to identify problems early on (and maybe fix them). Accordingly, here are some generic profiles of the different kinds of people who are often involved in estate disputes. This is not intended to stereotype or imply that all families with stepparents and stepchildren are destined for probate disputes—or for that matter, that all families without stepchildren or stepparents can expect trust and estate administration to be simple, straightforward, and guided by familial cooperation and understanding.

The Serial Litigator

Oftentimes a family will have a member or spouse of a member who is proud of filing lawsuits and either settling or winning. Perhaps he's sued various small businesses in town over minor issues. He even brags how he sued the city and won after tripping over an uneven sidewalk. Hitting others with meaningless lawsuits is a game he enjoys, and this family member is not above (or below) taking stepbrothers, stepsisters, or even his own siblings and parents to court for another miserable round of estate litigation. A Serial Litigator can be a real threat to an estate, particularly one who is indifferent to the potential consequence of most of the estate assets being consumed by attorneys' fees. The Serial Litigator's indifference may have little consequence to him but devastating financial consequences to his relatives.

Stepmother vs. stepchildren

Just as a reminder, I'm not implying any "evil stepmother" stereotype so familiar from fairy tales is related to probate litigation. Rather, my observations are merely indicative of the frequent conflicts in estate matters between stepmothers and stepchildren that I've come across. I've represented both sides, and I've seen how tensions in blended families can carry over into disputes over an inheritance, beneficiary rights to a trust, estate property, etc. At times there are even accusations of fraud and undue influence—claims to be determined through discovery in court.

The Amateur Google Legal Expert

We know how beneficial the Internet can be in solving all manner of problems, from simple home repair issues to language translation. Yet there are real limits to what the Internet can provide in the way of professional advice.

In the same way we can overreact by diagnosing ourselves via WebMD, it's not the best idea to craft an entire legal strategy from information gleaned from Google search results. In an estate dispute within a blended family, the Amateur Google Legal Expert will claim to other family members to have found the ultimate answer to their troubles and insist any lawyer who doesn't go along with the plan is a fool.[4]

While there are foolish lawyers out there, I'm confident that experience, training, and credibility in probate and trust litigation are worth their weight in gold. I would caution against embracing a legal strategy worked out by a nonprofessional armed with a mouse and three hours of Google time.

The 360-Degree Accuser

In blended-family estate disputes, this character appears on the scene with regularity, pointing a finger of blame at everyone but him- or herself. Maybe it's a stepbrother or stepsister who seems to find everything wrong with every other member of the family, leveling all sorts of accusations, from estate theft to undue influence and even murder. Now, all those nefarious acts do occasionally take place in estate cases, but somehow the 360-Degree Accuser manages to fit most of the family into an outrageous plot. The 360-Degree Accuser, meanwhile, is always totally innocent of any wrongdoing and would never be hiding something behind all his or her wild claims.

The Forgetter

This may be a stepparent or stepsibling who conveniently "forgets" the details of vital trust and estate documents or even where they were placed. The Forgetter might even hide the will, hoping that it will be flushed down the memory hole. Often this will coincide with the Forgetter taking family heirlooms, jewelry, cash, and other estate property, contrary to the terms of the will or trust. If the Forgetter is summoned for a deposition in trust or probate litigation, he or she will likely suffer "memory loss" on important points in the case. All that the Forgetter has concealed, however, will ultimately be revealed in the discovery process of estate litigation.

The Substance Abuser

The Substance Abuser is a common character in estate fights involving blended families. Many times, a family will have a "black sheep," and sometimes that child, or stepchild, will have a problem with substance abuse. Whether the issue is with alcohol, prescription drugs (a national challenge), or illegal narcotics, addiction is a debilitating condition that can generate further bad-faith behavior by the Substance Abuser, including conversion of estate funds and assets to fuel his or her drug habit. Entire family fortunes that took years to build can be flushed down the drain by the Substance Abuser. This fact should remind you to set up preventive measures in your estate plan sooner rather than later.

The Talker

My job is to help our clients and protect their interests. That means that I need the best possible accounting of all estate assets, with documentation a priority. With a blended family situation, however, things can get lost in the shuffle or even "forgotten" by bad actors looking to enrich themselves at others' expense (see the Forgetter, above). That's where the Talker comes in. A good probate-litigation attorney requires a clear view of all the funds and property of a trust or estate, but the Talker doesn't provide much help. The Talker will tell stories of hidden riches (big talk) or gossip about family members or neighbors (small talk), yet when it comes to flesh-and-blood estate matters, the Talker has little of substance to offer that would protect his or her interests.

The Screamer

The Screamer is easy to recognize in an estate fight between stepchildren/half children and stepparents—he or she raises the volume in the room all the way to 11, in the immortal words of Spinal Tap rocker Nigel Tufnel. While some people can understandably be frustrated by the outrageous behavior of an estate wrongdoer or the circumstances of the litigation process, the Screamer takes every opportunity to charge the atmosphere with unnecessary emotional tension and start a fight where there wasn't one to begin with. The Screamer is mostly about making noise, but without substantive facts, all the noise in the world won't prove anyone's status as a rightful trust beneficiary or heir to an estate.

The Simple Truth

The simple truth is that the estates of some fathers who leave a widowed stepmother and stepchildren will become battle-grounds. However small the percentage of such affected estates is, battleground estates can shift to hard-fought litigation that drains family fortunes and inflames emotions.[5]

When people call me about stepmother-stepchildren disputes, one of the first things I usually tell them is that cooler heads, willing to resolve matters early, will often save estate money and reduce the emotional and financial injury to all members of the decedent's family. Thankfully, there are still some good attorneys and reasonable clients who can achieve this goal. Meanwhile, those cases that escape early resolution often quickly escalate to probate, estate, trust, and property disputes that epitomize the stereotypes surrounding classic battles between stepmothers and their stepchildren.

Mediation as a Path to Resolution

Wronged heirs and abused beneficiaries often feel frustrated, believing that the system is rigged. After all, they've had a trust or estate hijacked from them through elder financial abuse, fraud, or some other form of malfeasance. Wrongdoer trustees may engage in wasteful trustee spending to defend their misdeeds at the cost of the trust—more accurately, at the cost of the wronged beneficiaries. It may take a good deal of time and a great deal of expense to finally get to a hearing or trial that can provide proof of wrongdoing. The realities of the underfunded California court system, which is constantly processing a heavy litigation caseload, inevitably raise the concern that justice delayed can truly be justice denied.[1]

Why Mediation?

Consequently, early mediation may be a more efficient, more effective approach for the disputing parties. So many times in life we need a referee. A referee helps us to save face and to overcome bitter, hardened positions that make resolution impossible. Estate, trust, and probate litigation often involves estate assets of real estate, cash, and securities. It's the attorney's job to recover what was wrongfully taken through exploitation, and sometimes the best route is through mediation. Client interests being paramount, at times a negotiated outcome is far superior to expensive and excruciating litigation.

Trust, probate, and estate litigation attorneys who challenge trustees, administrators, and executors provide their clients choices based upon the legal underpinnings of their case. Is there elder financial abuse? Is there undue influence? Has the trustee breached his duty to the trust beneficiaries, favoring his own interests over those who are supposed to benefit from the estate?

There are times when early mediation in trust litigation works very well. Of course, effective counsel will ensure that his or her clients are protected and prepared for the process. Inexperienced lawyers may view such offers of early mediation as a sign of weakness. Experienced lawyers, however, having spent a long time in the litigation ring, can use the process in the way a vaccine now prevents a long hospital stay later. A good doctor will tell you that inoculation is smarter, safer, and easier on the mind and body.[2]

In the same way, if you can avoid the stress of protracted litigation, an early mediation set soon after or even before litigation may be far more productive and emotionally satisfying than a settlement at the courthouse steps reached after two years of taxing litigation.

Mediation FAQs

Arm yourself with some simple truths about mediation and settlement:

- *What is mediation?* Mediation is the process by which a neutral person facilitates communications between two or more disputing parties to assist them in reaching a mutually acceptable agreement.[3]

- *Do settlement agreements have to be in writing?* A successful mediation is often documented at the end of the process by a summary agreement—sometimes called a term sheet—signed by all the parties. When this is not practical, and the parties otherwise agree, oral agreements can be made on the record and be followed by a record in writing. The California Probate Code allows the enforcement of such agreements that satisfy these conditions:

  > (a) The oral agreement is recorded by a court reporter or reliable means of audio recording.

  > (b) The terms of the oral agreement are recited on the record in the presence of the parties and the mediator, and the parties express on the record that they agree to the terms recited.

  > (c) The parties to the oral agreement expressly state on the record that the agreement is enforceable or binding, or words to that effect.

  > (d) The recording is reduced to writing and the writing is signed by the parties within 72 hours after it is recorded.[4]

- *Do courts require that parties mediate trust, estate, and probate disputes?* Estate litigators representing heirs and beneficiaries challenging California trusts and wills generally file the trust or will contest in the probate division of the superior court in which the decedent lived or the trust is being administered. Some cases are also filed in the civil division of the superior court. Courts overseeing such litigation often order the disputing parties to mediation. Such orders are made to force the parties to try to settle the inheritance lawsuit. Many times there are settlements reached in the superior courts.

I regularly represent parties in estate and trust disputes, many of which contain elements of elder financial abuse. Over the last few years, I have represented parties across California, from the Sierras to the Pacific coast. Of course, not all cases settle, and some cases may eventually proceed to trial. That said, in my experience, a sizable majority of cases are resolved prior to trial.

- ***Do all settlement agreements have to be approved by the court?*** Not all settlement agreements need to be approved by the court, but it is often a better practice to do so. Even absent court approval, a settlement agreement is a contract, and "a deal is a deal." Of course, the contract itself could provide that it is null and void if not approved by the court.

- ***Will courts enforce settlement agreements?*** When I represent clients who become parties to estate, trust, and probate settlement agreements, I make sure that the court retains jurisdiction over the settlement. In particular, I reference California Probate Code Section 664.6, which provides that "If requested by the parties, the court may retain jurisdiction over the parties to enforce the settlement until performance in full of the terms of the settlement." It makes little sense to get a settlement if it can't be enforced.

As a rule, discovery proceedings stop when there is a settlement agreement. This is something that should be addressed. The need to inform the court of the settlement should also be discussed, and a plan of action put in place.

Litigation, Mediation, and Your Privacy

In probate and elder financial abuse litigation, attorneys are called to represent client interests in full and minimize risk to client assets. Part of this mission is ensuring client privacy. No one wants his or her business, financial, or other information needlessly exposed to the public eye, and that's why a skilled attorney will design a trust to protect the privacy of an estate and its beneficiaries.[5]

A trust should be crafted with special attention to balancing interests, because once it's under dispute and subject to litigation, all bets are off. Privacy, a principle that almost all Americans highly value, often goes out the window when a case goes to court and the process of discovery begins. This is why our sixteenth president, Abraham Lincoln—himself an attorney—advised the following with regard to lawsuits and litigation:

> Discourage litigation. Persuade your neighbors to compromise whenever you can. As a peacemaker the lawyer has superior opportunity of being a good man. There will still be business enough.[6]

There are a number of options for steering clear of trust litigation and preserving the privacy of a trust. The initial composition of the trust document itself is the first line of defense against potential disruptions further along.

Sufficient flexibility in the structure of the trust, along with keeping beneficiaries informed of the ongoing distribution of assets, goes a long way in eliminating causes of conflict.

Appointment of a financial professional as trustee denotes fairness and impartiality in dealings with beneficiaries, and a trustee should be well versed in family dynamics to mitigate problems that might arise between parties.[7]

Peace of mind and client privacy are best secured when trust documents are initially drafted, but what happens if a trust comes into dispute? Lincoln's advice is still golden: There are ways to protect privacy and strike a decent compromise without stepping into a quagmire of costly and seemingly endless litigation.

As emphasized above, mediation, which is conducted in privacy and not subject to the public record, is a far preferable alternative to litigation. While mediation can in some instances be an intense process, it's certainly more cost-effective than litigation, plus it's free of all the attendant pressures of official court business. Attorneys in trust cases must be ready to do battle in probate litigation, but for the sake of client interests and privacy, there's a whole toolkit of options available to resolve a dispute before escalating to that final step.

Recognizing Different Styles of Opposing Counsels

Successful resolution of trust and estate litigation or a case of elder financial abuse is not always immediate. As a result, I often welcome early mediation. To the extent that my opposition views this as a weakness, so be it. As a practical matter, my client is not going to agree to something that doesn't make sense. I don't view mediation as exposing my client and myself to the dangers of Svengali, rendering us pawns in the scheme of an influential criminal mastermind. Mediation can be telling: It explores areas of common ground and identifies ultimate points of contention. Whether we reach resolution the same day or not, the opposing lawyer will display his or her style, and I take the time to note the strengths and weaknesses in my opponent's style.

While I have decades of experience confronting all kinds of lawyers on the opposite side of a dispute, during mediation my clients are usually seeing lawyers in action for the first time in their lives. Depictions they may have seen in movies and on television are seldom accurate, and the way lawyers behave in a real dispute often comes as a rude awakening. As a result, I try to prepare my clients ahead of time to identify certain "types" of opposing counsels and to understand that our ability to negotiate a positive outcome through mediation may depend, to some extent, upon what kind of attorney the other side has retained.

First, I confess to employing artistic license in my descriptions (below) of lawyers' advocacy styles that I've witnessed in the mediation of trust, estate, and elder financial abuse matters. Such license is meant to depict some real events, with the caveat that my analysis involves the reinterpretation of events, not literal portrayals. They're also subject to my own fallibilities in description and observation.

Second, I confess that the opposing lawyers I describe could write their own analyses of my style and place me within a classification that I might find, in a word, unflattering. I'm reminded of the wisdom of Matthew 7:3, "Why do you look at the speck of sawdust in your brother's eye and pay no attention to the plank in your own eye?" With that, let me start my analysis with the plank in my eye.

Lawyers' styles in mediation have real effects—real consequences for the mediation parties (including, of course, their own clients). The particular styles explored here are a regular part of the negotiation landscape for a skilled mediator. This skill consciously or unconsciously involves the subtle art of persuasion. A mediator is likely to make different arguments to me than an opponent in the same mediation. It is important in mediation that the mediator is able "to read" the mediation parties and their counsel. A good mediator can do this and will be very busy. A less skilled mediator may find his schedule too open for his own comfort.

This is not intended to be an exploration of antidotes or countermeasures to any particular advocacy style. It is simply a reflection on some of the opposing counsel styles that I have encountered in my many years of trust and financial elder abuse mediation.

The Rooster

The cock of the walk. When I sat down to write this reflection, the "Rooster" style came immediately to mind. The Rooster, or "cock of the walk," is a man who thinks he is stronger, more intelligent, and more successful than those around him. While the Rooster wants to be intimidating, at times he is just amusing. The Rooster enters mediation with an air of confidence that the mediator will serve him and his opponents will ultimately be subservient to his will. The Rooster purports to be an authority and an expert. As far as the Rooster is concerned, he is always the "elephant in the room."

The Insurance Adjuster

The Insurance Adjuster's style is that no matter what the value of a particular case, is it is important to protract negotiation and start at the lowest possible offer. Personally, I have little use for such a negotiating style and have terminated mediations where this behavior is exhibited. We take cases that we will mediate or try. The insurance adjuster simply facilitates our trial decision.

The Parasite

The parasitical approach is a variation of the "burn the house down" style of negotiating. The parasitical approach entails defending a particular claim by exhausting all the resources that would otherwise be available for settlement. This approach requires the defendant's or trustee's expressed willingness to spend all assets of an estate to defend against a claim. This tactic sometimes works, although there are countermoves. Real people with real injuries or inflicted wrongs can suffer because a trustee is willing "to burn the house down" rather than distribute a rightful share to the wronged beneficiary. Legal journals have addressed how sometimes law firm requirements for billable hours sometimes create pressures on partners and associates to overbill. Overbilling may involve over-lawyering a case: spending far more time than is necessary to handle a legal matter.

The Mockingbird

The Mockingbird makes fun of someone or something in a cruel way. Such behavior includes laughing at someone or something. Mockingbirds soon become infamous in the legal community. When you oppose a Mockingbird, you can expect that you and your client will be the subject of some derision. It is a real style, and for the most part it is offensive and dismissive of truth. The style is often noticeable in the Rooster.

The Jurist

The Jurist is an expert in or writer on law. The Jurist is often a legal scholar or legal theorist. I've seen cases where the opposing counsel is so focused on the law that other rules of advocacy are set aside. In the real world, juries don't make decisions based on a battle of professors. Juries address flesh-and-bone issues—what did someone lose as a result of wrongdoing? I usually enjoy opponents using the Jurist style because arguing over the law can be an engaging legal exercise. That said, the danger of the style is that the opponent "can't see the forest for the trees." The Jurist becomes so involved in the details of the problem that he cannot look at the situation as a whole.

The Soviet

The Soviet style of mediation negotiating involves extreme initial offers, expressions of limited authority, and stinginess. Such negotiating style assumes no continuing relationships because the style requires a "win-lose" approach. I've seen adherents of this style incorporate deception coupled with a complete lack of remorse for wrongdoing. The Soviet style often combines arrogance with rudeness. The Soviet style is cold and unpleasant.

These are just a few of the styles I routinely run into, but there are as many styles as opposing counsel. Again, the description of the various styles incorporates dramatic license. Still, for what it's worth, I must admit that when I am an advocate at mediation, I look for the telltale signs of the particular style that my opposing counsel embraces. I assume that he or she is looking at me in the same way.

Whatever the style, there are basic rules to live by as a lawyer, among them the ones expressed in the American Bar Association's Model Rules of Professional Conduct: Preamble & Scope:

> A lawyer's conduct should conform to the requirements of the law, both in professional service to clients and in the lawyer's business and personal affairs. A lawyer should use the law's procedures only for legitimate purposes and not to harass or intimidate others. A lawyer should demonstrate respect for the legal system and for those who serve it, including judges, other lawyers and public officials. While it is a lawyer's duty, when necessary, to challenge the rectitude of official action, it is also a lawyer's duty to uphold legal process.[8]

Financial Institutions and Their Roles in Fighting Elder Financial Abuse

In the fight against elder financial abuse, regulators and financial and legal professionals all need to partner for positive change. The exploitation of our senior citizens is already a serious threat to our local communities and national economy. The tremendous damage is reflected in local tragedies: the grandmother whose accounts were depleted by an unethical broker; the elderly man, suffering dementia, who was manipulated into changing his will by an unscrupulous relative; and the countless victims of any number of scams.

A 2015 speech on elder financial abuse by Kathleen Quinn, the executive director of the National Adult Protective Services Association (NAPSA), makes the gravity of this challenge all too clear. Addressing financial advisors from across the country at the prominent Senior Investors Forum in New York City, Quinn called on the crowd to protect their elderly clients from financial predators. While elder abuse is an insidious and growing phenomenon, Quinn noted that the resources to prevent it are limited.

To demonstrate the formidable struggle we face, she provided the following statistics to the audience:

- One in ten seniors—five million people—are victims of elder abuse and neglect every year. Quinn added that this adds up to more than the combined total of abused children (1.25 million) and battered women (2.3 million). We're witnessing a silent epidemic of crime.

- Reporting on elder abuse is nearly nonexistent, with only one in twenty-four cases ever reaching the authorities. Elder financial abuse is even less likely to be reported, with only one in forty-four cases coming to the attention of police or Adult Protective Services.

- The likelihood that victims of elder abuse will die within a few years is three times greater than it is with other senior citizens. Victims are also four times more likely to be put into a nursing home or care facility.

- Elder abuse is incredibly costly to all involved—the victims, their families, financial institutions, and taxpayers. The damage inflicted by elder financial abuse everywhere is in the multiple billions (according to recent research, anywhere from $3 billion to $36 billion).

- There is a lack of federal funding for the fight against elder financial abuse. Out of a requested $25 million, Congress appropriated $4 million for Adult Protective Services in 2015. Such funding is crucial for cash-strapped state and local Adult Protective Services agencies, which unfortunately cannot do very much without financial backing at the federal level.

- According to data from a 2012 NAPSA survey, 87 percent of state Adult Protective Services programs recorded an increase in reporting and caseloads. At the same time, half of the states cut spending to counter this ever-expanding crime wave.[1]

Quinn's statistics are clearly cause for alarm to American seniors and their loved ones. Whether we're family, financial professionals, caregivers, or attorneys, increased vigilance is necessary to prevent and stop elder financial abuse. Investment advisors and others working in the financial services industry have to be especially alert for signs of wrongdoing in their clients' account activity. That's why it's encouraging that both federal authorities and professional associations are stepping up their game against elder financial abuse.

FINRA Rules

In 2016, FINRA issued a new set of rules to clamp down on the growing problem of elder financial abuse. The agency's board of governors approved a proposal that enables financial services companies to place a temporary hold on the disbursement of funds from client accounts if there is a reasonable suspicion of exploitation. Richard Ketchum, FINRA's chief executive officer and chairman, remarked that FINRA's enactment of the new policy would help protect seniors from fraud, undue influence, and other damage wrought through elder financial abuse:

> Each day for the next 15 years, an average of 10,000 Americans will turn 65. Seniors are at risk, and FINRA is committed to helping protect seniors and other vulnerable adults from

financial exploitation. This proposal is an important step forward that would benefit both investors and firms.[2]

FINRA's new rule is crafted as an option for financial and investment planners, rather than a mandatory duty, until 2018, when it is to become official policy. The agency also has outlined a broad, commonsense definition of financial exploitation:

(4) For purposes of this Rule, the term "financial exploitation" means:

(A) the wrongful or unauthorized taking, withholding, appropriation, or use of a Specified Adult's funds or securities; or

(B) any act or omission by a person, including through the use of a power of attorney, guardianship, or any other authority regarding a Specified Adult, to:

(i) obtain control, through deception, intimidation or undue influence, over the Specified Adult's money, assets or property; or

(ii) convert the Specified Adult's money, assets or property.[3]

Under FINRA's guidelines, if a financial professional is concerned that an ill-intentioned third party is seeking access to a senior (sixy-five years and older) client's account, the professional can put a temporary hold on the transaction and seek to clarify the matter. Firms will be required to undertake "reasonable efforts" to obtain the name and telephone number of a trusted contact in case suspicious circumstances arise. Companies will also be legally shielded from liability for the holds, since such actions are to be taken in good faith for the benefit of the client and the service provider.

New policies to help protect seniors from elder financial abuse can't come soon enough, so FINRA's initiative is certainly welcome in light of continuing exploitation. For every story of elder financial abuse you see in the news, there might be a dozen cases that are never uncovered.

NASAA Guidelines

It is welcome news that more financial and investment professionals are becoming aware of the problem of elder financial abuse and taking concrete steps to combat it. Also in 2016, the North American Securities Administrators Association (NASAA) adopted new guidelines to help both regulators and advisors protect what it terms "vulnerable adults" (primarily the elderly) and prevent financial exploitation. NASAA president Judith Shaw remarked that the act "will help securities regulators, investment advisors, and broker-dealers, as well as Adult Protective Services agencies, work in partnership to protect our most vulnerable investors."[4]

Showing that it's done its homework on the threat of elder financial abuse, NASAA tells brokers and investment advisors to be alert for several signals that their elderly client might be the victim of manipulation or fraud. These red flags are drawn from the experience of professionals throughout the country and good old-fashioned common sense:

- Uncharacteristic and repeated cash withdrawals or wire transfers.

- Appearing with new and unknown associates, friends, or relatives.

- Uncharacteristic nervousness or anxiety when visiting the office or conducting telephonic transactions.

- Lacking knowledge about his or her financial status.

- [The financial advisor has] difficulty speaking directly with the client or customer without interference by others.

- Unexplained or unusual excitement about an unexplained or unusual windfall; reluctance to discuss details.

- Sudden changes to financial documents such as powers of attorney, account beneficiaries, wills, or trusts.

- Large, atypical withdrawals or closing of accounts without regard to penalties.[5]

In the spirit of FINRA's new rules, NASAA's model act allows brokers and advisors to delay disbursement of funds for up to fifteen days if they suspect wrongdoing afoot with a client account, plus an additional ten days on request of regulators or Adult Protective Services. If the financial professional does have reasonable suspicion of elder financial abuse or exploitation, he or she is required to report the case to state authorities, both the securities regulator and representatives of Adult Protective Services. Also, third parties initially designated by the client can be notified, as long as they're not a suspect in the abuse. To encourage responsible reporting, brokers and advisors are now given immunity from civil or administrative liability if they do take action to prevent potential exploitation.

The NASAA reporting procedure relies on a concise checklist of the facts in suspected cases of elder financial abuse, and it's useful to brokers as well as attorneys and family members of elders. It asks professionals to record the following information:

- the name of the client;

- the relevant dates;

- a description of the events that led to the report;

- a description of the steps the firm has taken or expects to take in response to the event; and

- any relevant documentation related to the potential financial exploitation to ensure that the internal stakeholders and any outside agency receiving the report has all of the necessary

- information to evaluate the report.[6]

The sooner information about an event is recorded and reported to proper authorities (whether it be law enforcement, Adult Protective Services, or regulators like FINRA), the better the chance that the wrongdoer will be held accountable. There's also a better chance for civil recovery when evidence and the accounts of victims are brought forward in a timely and organized manner.

CPA Financial Planners

A 2015 American Institute of Certified Public Accountants study interviewing 266 CPA financial planners found that two out of three professionals had encountered fraud or exploitation among their clients. For vulnerable elders, the anguish of victimization is often more painful than any amount of stolen money. Only 5 percent of clients reported substantial financial damage from elder abuse, but 37 percent said that the emotional toll inflicted by bad actors caused a "significant emotional impact."

Though the most common type of elder financial abuse reported in the study was perpetrated through phone or Internet scams, the reason for emotional scarring is likely due to wrongdoing committed closer to home. Seventy-two percent of advisors confirmed that they had come across cases of exploitation in which elders experienced an "inability to say no" to relatives demanding "loans," gifts, etc. Fifty-seven percent also cited "support" for non-disabled adult children as a type of abuse they've encountered among their clients. Indeed, the most serious form of elder financial abuse predominates within the family, and this would be the most emotionally wrenching situation to endure: when a loved one takes advantage of physical or mental incapacity, or simple kindness, to loot financial accounts and divert funds.

Nearly half (47 percent) of the planners noted an increase in elder financial abuse over the past five years. It's somewhat encouraging that only 5 percent of them had witnessed serious monetary damage from elder abuse, which shows that the system of checks and balances in place can work. Just imagine the ruin that financial predators bring upon those who don't have the benefit of a professional advisor, attorney, etc. who can spot potential fraud and assist in making sound financial decisions. Many senior citizens in our communities are already susceptible to undue influence, manipulation, and outright intimidation. If there's no one around to stop these behaviors, then not only the level of financial mayhem but also the level of misery rises. Protecting our elderly loved ones from harm isn't an option— it's our responsibility.[7]

Bank Tellers

According to a survey conducted by the Elder Protection Trust in 2010, around one out of five senior citizens has been or will be a victim of fraud.[8] Other figures don't leave room for much optimism; the National Adult Protective Services Association states that only about one in forty-four elders will end up reporting when they've been financially exploited. With such daunting odds in the fight against elder financial abuse, where is the best point to prevent it—or stop it in its tracks early on?

As it turns out, bank tellers are on the "front line" of the battle against elder financial abuse, since they are often the first to notice irregularities that might point to wrongdoing by a third party. An in-depth 2015 article in the *Bangor Daily News* highlights the important role of employees at local banks and credit unions in stopping the exploitation of our seniors.[9] An alert bank teller will often be able to spot the potential vulnerabilities of an elderly customer, as well as signs of financial foul play. Here are some red flags tellers should look out for:

- **Scams.** Seniors can easily fall victim to various telephone scams, bogus sweepstakes, and other frauds. Engaging the elderly customer in conversation and learning the purpose of their withdrawal could help protect their savings from financial predators.

- **Irregularities.** Irregularities in a senior customer's account could indicate that elder financial abuse is afoot. If the account is bouncing checks or overdrawn, then further investigation is warranted. Find out who else has access to the elder's account information. A reckless family member or another bad actor may be abusing his or her power of attorney over the elder's finances.

- **Vulnerabilities.** Tellers can watch for signs that an elderly customer's mental condition could be deteriorating, such as memory loss and other symptoms associated with dementia or Alzheimer's. Such ailments make seniors especially vulnerable to abusive predators.

In addition to spotting potential signs of trouble, bank tellers can also take positive steps against elder financial abuse. Whenever possible, bank tellers should encourage family involvement or enrollment in programs to help seniors manage their finances. In some cases, calling Adult Protective Services or the police may be necessary.

Special training for bank tellers can help detect and prevent elder financial abuse before it's too late. In Maine, for example, the public-private training program Senior$afe is equipping tellers with the knowledge and skills to protect their community's senior citizens from exploitation. Adoption of similar initiatives in California would go a long way in combating an epidemic of elder financial abuse in our state and restore an ethic of responsibility to financial services providers.[10]

Banks are key players in any effort to protect our seniors from wrongdoing. Bank and credit union personnel can make a significant, positive contribution in the fight against elder abuse, since they're frequently the first to spot that something is amiss in an elder's financial accounts. If a bank fails in its responsibility to protect senior citizens, it should be held accountable if found negligent or guilty of other offenses.

In certain cases, bank employees can also turn out to be perpetrators of elder financial exploitation, even cultivating relationships with elderly clients to exercise undue influence. When this occurs, the bank's management can choose between two basic steps: assisting the client in the recovery of funds or refusing to admit any liability and stonewalling. If a bank's higher-ups choose the latter course, they'll face litigation that could prove not only costly but a public relations disaster. The victims will convincingly argue that the bank should carry responsibility for the employee's reckless behavior and that there are no excuses for this system failure. If the bank doesn't reach a settlement, then let the jurors decide in civil court.

I am grateful for the opportunity to share some life experiences, strategies, and thoughts about the increasing dangers of elder financial abuse. After all that you have read, you now have the basics on how to approach an elder financial abuse action or family situation.

As countless stories in this book attest, challenging elder financial abuse often involves fighting a battle, and because the hurdles can be enormous, only a small percentage of abuse cases are ever filed or prosecuted. Family dynamics, issues of proof, and hubris limit active efforts to protect seniors or to recover against abusers. It can seem sometimes that inaction is safer than an active and uncomfortable challenge against a financial elder abuser.

How do you find the strength to challenge and protect against wrongdoers harming a living senior? Whatever religious or moral principles you embrace, consider the near-universal principle to "do unto others as you would have them do unto you." This is known as the Golden Rule.

If we apply the Golden Rule, we can decide how we would want to be treated if we found ourselves in a position vulnerable to the wrongdoing of others. Remember, we do not need to have incapacity to be vulnerable. Our particular vulnerability may be caused through illness, disability, injury, age, education, emotional distress, isolation, or dependency. Whatever our vulnerability, we will ultimately rely upon those who apply the Golden Rule to protect us when we cannot protect ourselves. We will be thankful for those souls who risk scorn and controversy to oppose wrongdoing.

My sincere hope is that this book gives you thoughts and strategies for addressing an existing elder financial abuse problem or prepares you to successfully respond to a future problem.

Acknowledgments

The Wolf at the Door is dedicated to my spouse, Lisa. Our long-time marriage and companionship is a continual source of joy and strength.

I particularly want to thank the following people who have helped make this book possible: Adam Rosen, my editor at AMR Editorial, for his care, expertise, and enthusiasm for my book; Mark Hackard, my son and compatriot, whose constant encouragement of me to write about the issues facing our senior population led me to a greater understanding of the widespread elder financial abuse that exists today; John Long, as a friend and for his indefatigable efforts in managing the day-to-day business of Hackard Law while I author a book, expand our geographic reach, and encourage our focus on excellence; and J.P. Mark, without whose encouragement and insight this book would not exist. Lastly, I thank my family, friends, and clients who have supported me in a long and fruitful legal career that I continue to enjoy after more than forty years of practice.

Notes

INTRODUCTION

[1] Richard J. Bonnie and Robert B. Wallace, eds., "Elder Mistreatment: Abuse, Neglect, and Exploitation in an Aging America," National Research Council (US) Panel to Review Risk and Prevalence of Elder Abuse and Neglect (2003), National Academies Press (US), doi: 10.17226/10406.

[2] MetLife Mature Market Institute, "The MetLife Study of Elder Financial Abuse: Crimes of Occasion, Desperation, and Predation Against America's Elders" (June 2011), accessed May 7, 2017, https://www.metlife.com/assets/cao/mmi/publications/studies/2011/mmi-elder-financial-abuse.pdf; Tobie Stanger, "Financial Elder Abuse Costs $3 Billion a Year. Or Is It $36 Billion?" Consumerreports.org, September 29, 2015, accessed May 7, 2017, http://www.consumerreports.org/cro/consumer-protection/financial-elder-abuse-costs--3-billion-----or-is-it--30-billion-.

[3] Cal. AB-140, Ch. 668, http://leginfo.legislature.ca.gov/faces/billNavClient.xhtml?bill_id=201320140AB140.

CHAPTER 1

[1] National Do Not Call Registry, accessed April 16, 2017, https://www.donotcall.gov/; "Finally! No more annoying robocalls and telemarketers," Nomorobo, accessed April 17, 2017, https://www.nomorobo.com.

CHAPTER 2

[1] James R. Knickman and Emily K. Snell, "The 2030 Problem: Caring for Aging Baby Boomers," *Health Services Research* 37 (2002): 849–88, doi: 10.1034/j.1600-0560.2002.56.x.

[2] Tony Schinella, "Portsmouth Police Sergeant Fired." *Portsmouth, NH Patch*, June 24, 2015, accessed April 17, 2017, http://patch.com/new-hampshire/portsmouthnh/portsmouth-police-sergeant-fired.

[3] Elizabeth Dinan, "Police Officer: 'I Was Watching a Crime,'" *Seacoastonline.com*, March 21, 2015, accessed April 17, 2017, http://www.seacoastonline.com/article/20150322/NEWS/150329856/101142/NEWS.

[4] Press release, Portsmouth Police Department, January 24, 2015, accessed April 17, 2017, http://www.cityofportsmouth.com/police/news062415a.pdf.

[5] Elizabeth Dinan, "Fired Cop Loses $2 million Inheritance," *Seacoastonline.com*, August 20, 2015, accessed April 17, 2017, http://www.seacoastonline.com/article/20150820/NEWS/15082985.

[6] David Robb, "A Cautionary Hollywood Tale: The Conman Who Stole Famed Art Director's Home—and the Sister Who Helped Him," *Deadline Hollywood*, July 23, 2015, accessed April 17, 2017, http://deadline.com/2015/07/conman-art-director-oscar-nominated-ross-bellah-hollywood-theft-1201483688/.

[7] David Robb, "Crook Who Stole Famed Art Director's House Confesses . . . Sort Of," *Deadline Hollywood*, July 31, 2015, accessed April 17, 2017, http://deadline.com/2015/07/ross-bellah-stolen-house-confession-crook-1201487688/.

[8] Danielle Radin. "Elder Abuse Case: Neighbors Thought She Died Years Ago," *KRCRTV.com*, May 13, 2016, accessed April 17, 2017, http://www.krcrtv.com/news/local/shasta/elder-abuse-case-neighbors-thought-she-died-years-ago/11260578; Jim Schultz, "Murder Trial Date Set for Redding Mom and Daughter," *Redding Record Searchlight*, December 22, 2016, accessed April 17, 2017, http://www.redding.com/story/news/local/2016/12/21/murder-trial-date-set-redding-mom-and-daughter/95715380/.

[9] Ashley Cullins, "Sumner Redstone Sues Ex-Companions for Elder Abuse to Reclaim $150M in Gifts," *The Hollywood Reporter*, October 25, 2016, accessed April 17, 2017, http://www.hollywoodreporter.com/thr-esq/sumner_redstone-sues-companions-elder-abuse-reclaim-150m-gifts-937749.

[10] Keach Hagey and Joe Flint, "Sumner Redstone's National Amusements to Call on Viacom and CBS to Explore Merger," *Wall Street Journal*, September 28, 2016, accessed April 17, 2017, http://www.wsj.com/articles/sumner-redstones-national-amusements-to-call-on-viacom-and-cbs-to-explore-merger-1475077902; Mike Hackard, "Undue Influence Alleged in Sumner Redstone Estate Battle," Hackard Law blog, February 19, 2016, accessed April 17, 2017, http://www.hackardlaw.com/blog/2016/02/undue-influence-alleged-in-sumner-redstone-estate-battle.shtml; Mike Hackard, "Sumner Redstone: Incapacity & Undue Influence," Hackard Law blog, January 20, 2016, accessed April 17, 2017, http://www.hackardlaw.com/blog/2016/01/sumner-redstone-incapacity-undue-influence.shtml.

[11] Meg James, "Sumner Redstone Says Ex-Girlfriends Made Off With $150 Million, Leaving Him 'in Debt,'" *Los Angeles Times*, October 25, 2016, accessed April 17, 2017, http://www.latimes.com/entertainment/envelope/cotown/la-et-ct-sumner-redstone-elder-abuse-suit-20161025-snap-story.html.

[12] Complaint and Demand for Jury Trial, *Redstone v. Herzer et. al.*, No. BC 638054 (*Los Angeles Cty. Sup. Ct.* Oct. 25, 2016), hosted on Hackardlaw.com, accessed April 17, 2017, http://www.hackardlaw.com/blog/images/Sumner%20Redstone%20Elder%20Abuse%20Suit.pdf.

CHAPTER 3

[1] Sandee LaMotte, "Alzheimer's Diagnosis Hidden by Doctors," CNN.com, June 25, 2015, accessed April 17, 2017, http://www.cnn.com/2015/03/25/health/alzheimers-diagnosis/.

[2] Mike Hackard, "Alzheimer's | California Estate, Probate & Trust Litigation" Hackard Law blog, November 14, 2016, accessed April 17, 2017, http://www.hackardlaw.com/blog/2016/11/alzheimers-california-estate-probate-trust-litigation.shtml.

[3] Mike Hackard, "Mental Illness | Contesting a California Will or Trust," Hackard Law blog, September 27, 2016, accessed April 17, 2017, http://www.hackardlaw.com/blog/2016/09/mental-illness-contesting-a-california-will-or-trust.shtml.

[4] Lamotte, "Alzheimer's Diagnosis Hidden by Doctors."

[5] Mason Braswell, "Finra Files Complaint Against Broker for Trying to Inherit $1.8M from Client with Alzheimer's," *InvestmentNews*, June 12, 2015, accessed April 13, 2017, http://www.investmentnews.com/article/20150612/FREE/150619960/finra-files -complaint-against-broker-for-trying-to-inherit-1-8m-from.

[6] Hackard, "Mental Illness | Contesting a California Will or Trust."

[7] Cordula Dick-Muehlke, "Mental Health Services for Californians with Alzheimer's Disease," Alzheimer's Association report, 2016, accessed April 17, 2017, http://www.chhs.ca.gov/Alzheimer/Agenda%20Item%203-%20Mental%20Health %20Access%20for%20Persons%20with%20Dementia%20FINAL%20PAPER.pdf.

[8] Bradford, Andrea et al, "Missed and Delayed Diagnosis of Dementia in Primary Care: Prevalence and Contributing Factors," *Alzheimer Disease Associated Disorders* 23.4 (2009): 306–314, doi: 10.1097/WAD .0b013e3181a6bebc.

[9] N. R. Kleinfield, "Fraying at the Edges: Her Fight to Live With Alzheimer's," *New York Times*, April 30, 2016, accessed April 17, 2017, http://www.nytimes.com /interactive/2016/05/01/nyregion/living-with-alzheimers.html.

[10] Mike Hackard, "Undue Influence in Estate Litigation: 2016 Trends," Hackard Law blog, May 6, 2016, accessed April 17, 2017, http://www.hackardlaw.com/blog/2016 /05/undue-influence-in-estate-litigation-2016-trends.shtml.

[11] Mike Hackard, "Diagnosing Alzheimers | Protecting Estate Assets," Hackard Law blog, November 17, 2016, accessed April 17, 2017, http://www.hackardlaw.com/blog /2016/11/diagnosing-alzheimers-protecting-estate-assets.shtml.

[12] Cal. Prob. Code § 811, http://leginfo.legislature.ca.gov/faces/codes_displaySection .xhtml?sectionNum=811.&lawCode=PROB.

[13] Sam Naimi, "Robin Williams' Widow Seeks Clarification of Trust Terms," Wealth Management.com, June 4, 2015, accessed April 17, 2017, http://www.wealthmanage ment.com/high-net-worth/robin-williams-widow-seeks-clarification-trust-terms.

CHAPTER 4

[1] Mike Hackard, "The Widowed Stepmother | Big Trust and Estate Fights," Hackard Law blog, November 10, 2016, accessed April 17, 2017, http://www.hackard law.com/blog/2015/11/stepmother-trust-estate-fights-ahead.shtml.

[2] Cal. Prob. Code § 10811, http://leginfo.legislature.ca.gov/faces/codes_display Section.xhtml?sectionNum=10811.&lawCode=PROB.

[3] ESTATE OF GUERIN, 194 Cal.App.2d 566 (Cal. Ct. App. 1961), https://casetext .com/case/estate-of-guerin.

[4] "Current Rules: Rule 4-200 Fees for Legal Services," State Bar of California, 2016, http://rules.calbar.ca.gov/Rules/RulesofProfessionalConduct/CurrentRules /Rule4200.aspx.

[5] Evan L. Loeffler, "How to Avoid the Surprise Attorney-Client Relationship," *GPSOLO*, July/August 2010, accessed April 17, 2017, http://www.american bar.org/content/newsletter/publications/gp_solo_magazine_home/gp_solo_magazine_ index/solo_lawyer_ethics_attorney_client_relationship.html.

[6] Gabriel Tynes, "Coffee Heirs Ordered to Pay Attorneys More than $13 Million," *Lagniappe Mobile*, October 9, 2015, accessed April 17, 2017, http://lagniappe mobile.com/coffee-heirs-ordered-pay-attorneys-13-million/.

[7] Order for Attorneys' Fees, *Hill v. Estate of Leroy Hill,* No. CV-2014-900513.00 (Mobile Cty. Circ. Court, Oct. 7, 2015), https://assets.documentcloud.org/documents /2454376/2015-10-07-order-on-atty-fees.pdf.

CHAPTER 5

[1] Charles Swindoll, "Attitude," design.caltech.edu, accessed April 17, 2017, http://www.design.caltech.edu/erik/Misc/Attitude.html.

[2] Sun Tzu, *The Art of War,* The Internet Classics Archive, accessed April 17, 2017, http://classics.mit.edu/Tzu/artwar.html.

[3] "OODA Loops: Understanding the Decision Cycle," MindTools, accessed April 17, 2017, https://www.mindtools.com/pages/article/newTED_78.htm.

[4] Harry Hillaker, "Tribute To John R. Boyd," *Code One Magazine,* July 1997, accessed April 17, 2017, http://www.codeonemagazine.com/article.html?item_id=156.

[5] "Pulmonary Hypertension—High Blood Pressure in the Heart-to-Lung System," American Heart Association, last modified December 14, 2016, accessed April 17, 2017, http://www.heart.org/HEARTORG/Conditions/HighBloodPressure/About HighBloodPressure/What-is-PulmonaryHypertension_UCM_301792_Article.jsp#. VstqyGf2aUk.

[6] Gregory Brown, "The Doctrine of Laches," Avvo guide, August 1, 2011, accessed April 17, 2017, https://www.avvo.com/legal-guides/ugc/the-doctrine-of-laches.

CHAPTER 6

[1] *Intrieri v. Superior Court,* 117 Cal. App. 4th 72, (2004), http://caselaw.find law.com/ca-court-of-appeal/1010066.html.

[2] Mike Hackard, "Trying to Hide the Will? We'll See About That," Hackard Law blog, September 17, 2015, accessed April 17, 2017, http://www.hackardlaw.com/blog /2015/09/trying-to-hide-a-will-well-see-about-that.shtml.

[3] Cal. Civ. Code § 3294, https://leginfo.legislature.ca.gov/faces/codes_displaySection .xhtml?lawCode=CIV&sectionNum=3294.

[4] Cal. Civ. Code § 1209(a)(5), https://leginfo.legislature.ca.gov/faces/codes_display Section.xhtml?lawCode=CCP&sectionNum=1209.

CHAPTER 7

[1] "Elder Abuse," National Committee for the Prevention of Elder Abuse, accessed April 17, 2017, http://www.preventelderabuse.org/elderabuse/fin_abuse.html.

[2] Cal. WIC Code § 15610.70, https://leginfo.legislature.ca.gov/faces/codes_display Section.xhtml?lawCode=WIC&sectionNum=15610.70.

[3] Ibid.

[4] Michael LaMay, "Undue Influence Defined: New Statutory Definition and Recent Case Law," *Contra Costa Lawyer Online,* April 1, 2014, accessed April 17, 2017, http://cclawyer.cccba.org/2014/04/undue-influence-defined-new-statutory-definition -and-recent-case-law/.

[5] Cal. WIC Code § 15610.70.

[6] Ibid.

[7] Mike Hackard, "How Do I Find A Probate or Trust Litigation Attorney Near Me?" Hackard Law blog, August 25, 2016, accessed April 17, 2017, http://www.hackard law.com/blog/2016/08/how-do-i-find-a-probate-or-trust-litigation-attorney-near-me .shtml.

[8] Cal. AB-140, Ch. 668.

CHAPTER 8

[1] Emma Cook, "I Love Him, but Not His Kids," *Guardian*, March 10, 2007, accessed April 17, 2017, http://www.theguardian.com/lifeandstyle/2007/mar/10/familyand relationships.family1.

[2] "Clinical Dementia Rating (CDR)," Knight Alzheimer's Disease Research Center, table, accessed May 16, 2017, http://knightadrc.wustl.edu/cdr/PDFs/CDR_Table.pdf.

[3] Andrea Coombes, "How to Avoid Estate Fights among Your Heirs," *Wall Street Journal*, December 15, 2013, accessed April 17, 2017, http://www.wsj.com /articles/SB10001424052702303932504579252593886768168.

[4] Mike Hackard, "Do-It-Yourself Estate Law," Hackard Law blog, May 21, 2015, accessed April 17, 2017, http://www.hackardlaw.com/blog/2015/05/do-it-yourself -estate-law.shtml.

[5] Tessa Berenson, "Robin Williams' Widow Opens Up about Estate Battle," *Time*, November 5, 2015, accessed April 17, 2017, http://time.com/4101691/robin-williams -widow-estate-fight/.

CHAPTER 9

[1] Darrell Smith, "State Judicial Council: 'We Are Out of Money' for Court Construction," *Sacramento Bee*, September 16, 2016, accessed April 17, 2017, http://www .sacbee.com/news/business/article99715442.html.

[2] Mary F. Radford, *Advantages and Disadvantages of Mediation in Probate, Trust, and Guardianship Matters* , 1 Pepp. Disp. Resol. L.J. Iss. 2 (2001), http://law .pepperdine.edu/dispute-resolution-law-journal/issues/volume-one/11-radford.pdf.

[3] Cal. Prob. Code § 1115, http://leginfo.legislature.ca.gov/faces/codes_displayText .xhtml?lawCode=EVID&division=9.&chapter=2.&article.

[4] Cal. Prob. Code § 118, http://leginfo.legislature.ca.gov/faces/codes_displayText .xhtml?lawCode=EVID&division=9.&chapter=2.&article.

[5] Steven Seidenberg, "Plotting Against Probate," *ABA Journal*, May 1, 2008, accessed April 17, 2017, http://www.abajournal.com/magazine/article/plotting_against_pro bate/.

[6] Eric Svane, letter to the editor, *New York Times*, June 19, 1991, accessed April 17, 2017, http://www.nytimes.com/1991/07/12/opinion/l-persuade-your-neighbors-to -compromise-218791.html.

[7] Mike Hackard, "Resolving CA Trust Disputes | Establishing Order from Chaos," Hackard Law blog, January 5, 2017, accessed April 17, 2017, http://www.hackardlaw .com/blog/2017/01/resolving-ca-trust-disputes-establishing-order-from-chaos.shtml.

[8] "Model Rules of Professional Conduct: Preamble & Scope," American Bar Association—Center for Professional Responsibility, accessed April 17, 2017, http://www.americanbar.org/groups/professional_responsibility/publications/model_rules_of_professional_conduct/model_rules_of_professional_conduct_preamble_scope.html.

CHAPTER 10

[1] Bernice Napach, "As Elder Abuse Grows, Advisors Urged to Start Fighting It: SIFMA Forum," *ThinkAdvisor*, October 14, 2015, accessed April 17, 2017, http://www.thinkadvisor.com/2015/10/14/as-elder-abuse-grows-advisors-urged-to-start-fight; William F. Benson, Elder Justice Coordinating Council testimony, National Adult Protective Services Association, October 5, 2016, accessed May 8, 2017, http://www.napsa-now.org/wp-content/uploads/2016/10/EJCC-Testimony.pdf.

[2] "FINRA Board Approves Rulemaking Item to Protect Seniors and Other Vulnerable Adults from Financial Exploitation," press release, FINRA.org, September 17, 2015, accessed April 17, 2017, http://www.finra.org/newsroom/2015/finra-board-approves-rule-protecting-seniors-financial-exploitation.

[3] "2165. Financial Exploitation of Specified Adults," *FINRA Manual*, adopted March 9, 2016, accessed April 17, 2017, http://finra.complinet.com/en/display/display_main.html?rbid=2403&element_id=12784.

[4] Melanie Waddell, "NASAA Adopts Model Rule to Fight Senior Financial Abuse," *ThinkAdvisor*, February 1, 2016, accessed April 17, 2017, http://www.thinkadvisor.com/2016/02/01/nasaa-adopts-model-rule-to-fight-senior-financial.

[5] "Detecting Senior Financial Exploitation," Serve Our Seniors, accessed April 17, 2017, http://serveourseniors.org/about/industry/practices-procedures-guide/detecting-senior-financial-exploitation/.

[6] "Reporting Senior Financial Exploitation," Serve Our Seniors, accessed April 17, 2017, http://serveourseniors.org/about/industry/practices-procedures-guide/reporting-senior-financial-exploitation/.

[7] Megan Leonhardt, "More Emotional Harm Than Financial in Elder Fraud," *Wealth Management.com*, June 23, 2015, accessed April 17, 2017, http://www.wealthmanagement.com/client-relations/more-emotional-harm-financial-elder-fraud.

[8] "Elder Investment Fraud and Financial Exploitation: A Survey Conducted for Investor Protection Trust," infogroup/ORC report, June 15, 2010, accessed April 17, 2017, http://www.investorprotection.org/downloads/EIFFE_Survey_Report.pdf.

[9] Erin Rhoda, "The Frontlines of Elder Financial Exploitation," *Bangor Daily News*, 2015, accessed April 17, 2017, http://external.bangordailynews.com/projects/2015/04/financial-exploitation/#.VVDvi2d0yUk.

[10] Senior$afe educational brochure, Maine Council for Elder Abuse Prevention, January 4, 2016, accessed April 17, 2017, http://elderabuseprevention.info/sites/default/files/Senior$afe_Materials_01.04.16.pdf.

Index

abuse. *See* elder financial abuse;
    physical abuse
accounting, 33–34, 81, 127–28
acquisition, wrongful, 78–79
Adelman, Herb, 34
Adult Protective Services, 16, 18,
    34, 121–23, 125, 126, 127,
    130
Alabama, 60–61
alcohol abuse, 89, 96, 108–9
*Alzheimer Disease & Associated
    Disorders* (journal), 42–43
Alzheimer's Association, 39, 40,
    42
Alzheimer's disease, 39–50
    concealment of, 39, 40, 45–46
    determining capacity, 46 47,
        79, 95–97
    diagnosing, 40, 42–43
    documenting, 44–46
    increase in people with, 42–44
    legal cases, 41–50, 103–4
    stigma of, 39
    susceptibility and, 88
    undue influence and, 40–47, 49
American Bar Association, 120
American Institute of Certified
        Public Accountants
        (AICPA), 127–28
antivirus scams, 25
anxiety, feelings of, 4–6
Arizona, 41–42
assets, misappropriation of, 78–79
assets, vanishing, 19

assisted living centers, transfers
    to, 17–18
attorneys, 51–62
    advocacy styles of, 116–20
    client privacy, 115–16
    fees, 10, 56–62
    locating, 51–55
    professional conduct of, 120
    responsibility of, 5, 51–52
    second opinions, 49
    See also litigation strategy
authority, 7, 19, 92
Avvo, 55

bank accounts
    email scams, 21–23
    oversight of, 13, 27
    sweepstakes scams, 26
    unexplained withdrawals, 19
bank tellers, role of, 128–31
Banner Alzheimer's Institute, 40
Behr, Peter, 53–54, 55
Bellah, Eunice, 33-34
Bellah, Ross, 33–34
bills, unpaid, 18–19, 20
blended families. *See* stepmothers
    /stepchildren
Boyd, John, 68–69, 72
BrokerCheck, 23
burden of proof, 87–88
burial arrangements, 105

California Adult Protective
    Services, 16, 34

About the Author

MICHAEL HACKARD is the founder of Hackard Law, a California law firm that focuses on estates and trusts litigation. Over the years, he has helped many victims of elder financial abuse, including trust beneficiaries, disinherited heirs, and relatives of family members. He practiced law for more than forty years before writing *The Wolf at the Door* and has an "AV Rating" from Martindale-Hubbell® Peer Review, signifying the highest level of professional excellence. He has been interviewed regularly by local and national media, including the *Wall Street Journal*, C-SPAN, and Fox News, and has testified before the House of Representatives.

Mike received his JD from the McGeorge School of Law and has been a member of the California Bar Association since 1976. He lives in Sacramento, California, and can be contacted at hackard@hackardlaw.com.

To learn more about Mike and elder financial abuse, please visit www.hackardlaw.com.

Please send all media- or publicity-related inquiries to Mark Hackard at mark.hackard@hackardlaw.com.

Made in the USA
Las Vegas, NV
03 August 2023

75586955R00100